Navigating the Phases of Sex Addiction Recovery

Designed for use with clients recovering from sex addiction, this book guides readers through discovering the essential skills for their sober journey and finding meaning and purpose in life through character development and emotional maturity, while improving their relationship with healthy intimacy.

This workbook answers the question, "I'm sober, now what?". It contains concise exercises and takes the reader on a journey that will give them an insight into what is holding them back from a life worth living, finally living in serenity, learning the art of surrender, and finding true hope and freedom in recovery. With alternating chapters presenting problems and solutions, this workbook is designed to lead the reader through the stages of recovery while gaining skills in mindfulness, emotional regulation, and impulse control.

Allan J. Katz is a Licensed Professional Counselor (LPC/MHSP) working as private practitioner in Memphis, Tennessee, and a Certified Sex Addiction Therapist.

Navigating the Phases of Sex Addiction Recovery

A Workbook for Adding Meaningful Value and Purpose to Sobriety

Allan J. Katz

Routledge
Taylor & Francis Group

NEW YORK AND LONDON

Designed cover image: © Getty

First published 2024
by Routledge
605 Third Avenue, New York, NY 10158

and by Routledge
4 Park Square, Milton Park, Abingdon, Oxon, OX14 4RN

Routledge is an imprint of the Taylor & Francis Group, an informa business

© 2024 Allan J. Katz

Library of Congress Cataloging-in-Publication Data
Names: Katz, Allan J., author.
Title: Navigating the phases of sex addiction recovery : a workbook for adding meaningful value and purpose to sobriety / Allan J. Katz.
Description: New York, NY : Routledge, 2024. | Includes bibliographical references and index.
Identifiers: LCCN 2023039602 (print) | LCCN 2023039603 (ebook) | ISBN 9781032684543 (hbk) | ISBN 9781032591421 (pbk) | ISBN 9781003453185 (ebk)
Subjects: LCSH: Sex addiction--Treatment. | Sex addicts--Rehabilitation.
Classification: LCC RC560.S43 K388 2024 (print) | LCC RC560.S43 (ebook) | DDC 616.85/833--dc23/eng/20231002
LC record available at https://lccn.loc.gov/2023039602
LC ebook record available at https://lccn.loc.gov/2023039603

ISBN: 9781032684543 (hbk)
ISBN: 9781032591421 (pbk)
ISBN: 9781003453185 (ebk)

DOI: 10.4324/9781003453185

Typeset in Times New Roman
by KnowledgeWorks Global Ltd.

Dedicated to the memory of Emily G.—A prolific writer whose precious life was cut short by addiction.

Contents

Biographical Sketch

Allan J. Katz

Allan J. Katz is a Licensed Professional Counselor (LPC/MHSP) in the state of Tennessee and a Certified Sex Addiction Therapist, Certified by IITAP, the International Institute for Trauma and Addiction Professionals. He is currently in private practice in Memphis, Tennessee, after serving as an individual and group therapist in an alcohol and drug treatment center for six years.

He treats compulsive behaviors and addictions (substance and process addictions—including sex/love/romance, gambling, and work-related addictions; all aspects of sexuality, trauma (including PTSD and betrayal trauma), anxiety disorders, codependency, family issues, life transitions, and mood disorders.

Allan is the author of four books: Addictive Entrepreneurship, dealing with the 13 traits needed to overcome work-related addictions, and Experiential Group Therapy Interventions with DBT: A 30-day program for treating addictions and trauma. He coauthored *Help Her Heal* with Carol Sheets and *Ambushed by Betrayal* with Michele Saffier.

Allan has received additional training in Neuro-linguistic Programming, Trauma Counseling, Brainspotting, Emotionally Focused Couples Therapy, The Developmental Model of Couples Therapy, and Experiential Therapy. He is a member of the American Counseling Association and Chairman of the Products Committee at the Association for Specialists in Group Work.

Preface

Allan J. Katz

This book is for the person in recovery from sex addiction, designed to help you maintain your sobriety by solving problems and providing tools for managing distractions, impulsivity, and indifference that could take you down a slippery slope toward relapse.

Navigating the phases of sex addiction recovery explores the elements that distract you today and the gentle path toward real hope, true freedom, and emotional integrity, adding value and purpose to living a sober life.

When you put in the work and do the exercises in this workbook, you'll discover how to temper out-of-control emotions. You'll discover how to begin to trust and protect others. You'll discover the fine line between letting technology waste your precious time while balancing it with healthy play. And you'll discover how to transform your life into being a human being instead of a human doing.

How to Use This Workbook

This book is for the person in recovery from sex addiction, designed to help you maintain your sobriety by solving problems and providing tools for managing distractions, impulsivity, and indifference that could take you down a slippery slope toward relapse. Complacency will rear its ugly head, and the exercises in this workbook will prepare you to face any challenge that lies ahead.

Recovery from sex addiction is a process, like an up-and-down roller coaster—that never stops. There is never a finite endpoint at which you can say, "That's it. I'm cured." There will always be hurdles that come up during recovery that challenge your progress and the assumptions that led you to sobriety. Those difficult moments can set you back, as they may have set you back many times. But when you're armed with the knowledge that these challenges will come up—and you're prepared with concrete strategies to face them—you can face any challenge that comes your way.

These hurdles represent times when we have to overcome distractions, indifference, and impulsivity in order to find meaning and purpose in our lives.

These hurdles can be grouped into six categories…

SECTION ONE: TECHNOLOGY
SECTION TWO: WORK
SECTION THREE: EMOTIONS
SECTION FOUR: PEOPLE
SECTION FIVE: SEXUALITY AND INTIMACY
SECTION SIX: TOOLS FOR MANAGING YOUR LIFE

Within each section, we will tackle these hurdles by first explaining the background of each one and why it comes up…

Then we'll go through specific tools and strategies to prepare you for maintaining your sobriety as you encounter each hurdle…

Navigating the Phases of Sex Addiction Recovery explores the elements that distract you today and the gentle path toward real hope, true freedom, and emotional integrity, adding value and purpose to living a sober life.

Here's what you'll discover when you purchase this workbook

When you put in the work and do the exercises in this workbook, you'll discover how to temper out-of-control emotions. You'll discover how to begin to trust and protect others. You'll discover the fine line between letting technology waste your precious time while balancing it with healthy play. And you'll discover how to transform your life into being a human being instead of a human doing. And by getting to know yourself better, you'll finally enjoy meaning and purpose in your life, knowing you're living up to higher values.

To live a value-led life, understand that you can enjoy freedom even with restrictions and rules, when the restrictions and rules are specifically designed to bring you closer to your own authentic self through spirituality, trust, mindfulness, and play.

What is Addiction?

In this workbook, we will refer to an obsession with unhealthy behaviors as "addiction," while presenting the character traits needed to extinguish "defects of character" as described in 12-step programs such as Alcoholics Anonymous, Sex and Love Addicts Anonymous, Sexaholics Anonymous, Recovering Couples Anonymous, and Sex Addicts Anonymous.

Addiction is defined as an obsessive-compulsive behavior that a person tries to stop and continues to occur despite his best efforts to stop on his own. Life then spins out of control and begins to affect his money, job, relationships, and health. It's really a reliance on a substance, process, or behavior that continues, despite dire and dangerous consequences.

Curious whether you might have an addiction?

See the Appendix for Addiction Assessments.

Section I

Technology

Chapter 1

The Tech Wreck Distractor

I Distract Myself to Avoid My Feelings, Family, and Friends

In years past only medical professionals and emergency workers had beepers that alerted them to an emergency. Today all of you have cellphones, and every call alert becomes an emergency. A person can be in the middle of prayer or meditation, and if his phone dings, he will interrupt his dialogue with God to answer his phone. After all, who is more important, me or God? Usually, it's his wife texting or emailing him to go pick up some groceries on his way home.

Psychologically it's all about ego. A person says to himself, *I am so important that I might miss something that I've been waiting for, for several years, so I interrupt what I'm doing and answer the phone.* We become obsessed with the notion that whatever we're doing now is not as important as what may be on the other end of that phone, even if it's 6:30 in the morning.

Every bit of technology has its benefits and drawbacks. What hinders you is our need for instant gratification and the possibility of finally fulfilling our dreams of wealth and happiness. Yet sooner or later we're up late at night playing video games because we can't sleep from the stresses of the day, and we still are not happy, wealthy, or fulfilled.

Fomo Activity

A client wrote, *I have to be friends with everyone on Facebook, I don't want to be rejected or excluded. I smoke weed because all my friends do it. I end up doing things I may not believe in or want to do so I just join in.*

People struggle sometimes with not being able to say no to something or someone. This could be part of addiction where they don't want to miss out on the next high or be an example of people pleasing; saying yes to things when they really want to say no. The remedy is to devote their time and energy to other more beneficial, useful activities.

What do you fear you're missing out on? _____

How does technology feed into your desire to fit in? _____

What do you commonly say yes to, when really you want to say no? (Food, sex, alcohol, drugs, gambling, shopping for what you WANT instead of what you might NEED, etc.)
_____

What will be different when you stand up for what YOU want and not just join in because everyone else is doing it? _____

DOI: 10.4324/9781003453185-2

Technology Checklist

Mark as many as are applicable and answer the questions below:

q.   Texting
r.   Sexting
s.   Pornography, Video Chat
t.   Video Games
u.   Dating Apps
v.   Social Media: Facebook, Instagram
w.   Sports
x.   News
y.   Weather
z.   TV
aa. Movies
bb. Gambling Online
cc. Video Sites: YouTube, TikTok

The benefit I get from technology is? _____

I fear if I spend less time on the Internet, I will miss _____.

Describe what's missing in your life that you "have to" spend time engaging in sexting, pornography, chatting, dating apps (when you're not really dating). _____

_____

If you don't stay current with the latest news and weather, what is the worst that will happen?

_____

How often has it happened? _____

On social media, are you comparing yourself with others? If so, what benefit are you getting? You would not be doing it if there was not some benefit! _____

_____

Cellphone Addiction

According to Jamison Monroe, CEO and Founder of Newport Academy, *Each (social media) 'like' increases dopamine, just as cocaine and other drugs do. In adolescents, the brain is rapidly developing, and the pleasure centers are all coming on board. Then, when teens derive addictive pleasures from social media, it can be a recipe for ignoring real-world pleasures, such as building true person-to-person relationships*

Research by the National Institute of Health hypothesized that social media use predicted reductions in positive affect and elevations in negative affect. However, contrary to expectations, social media use was not found to predict self-esteem or paranoia. Further analyses revealed that posting about daily activities (e.g., Facebook, Instagram, etc.) predicted high positive affect and self-esteem, whereas posting about feelings and venting on social media predicted low positive affect, low self-esteem, high negative affect, and paranoia.

Moreover, these surveys showed that adolescents who spent more time on social media were more likely to report mental health issues. Meanwhile, teens who spent more time on non-screen activities, such as in-person social interaction, sports, exercise, homework, and print media, were less likely to report mental health issues.

According to Pew Research Center study, April–May, 2022, 54% of teens say it would be hard to give up social media. Forty-five percent of teen girls and 32% of teen boys say social media makes them feel overwhelmed by drama, excluded by friends, or worse about their life. Teens are more likely to view social media as having a negative effect on others rather than themselves. However, a majority of teens report it increases their social connection and feeling of being included.

Stats of Adult Usage

A Pew Research Study in 2021 reported that 84% of adults ages 18–29 say they ever use any social media sites, which is similar to the share of those ages 30–49 who say this (81%). By comparison, a somewhat smaller share of those ages 50–64 (73%) say they use social media sites, while fewer than half of those 65 and older (45%) report doing this.

Resources for Parents and Teens http://culturereframed.com

How Technology Affects Us

David Henninger, writing in the *Wall Street Journal*, Aug. 8, 2019, says, "Whether the adaptability of the human brain is the invention of God or Darwin, I don't think it was designed to endure the volume of relentless inner-directedness that is driven by computerized devices and cellphone screens. It is not natural or normal." Young women are comparing themselves to photoshopped images of "perfect" supermodels and other students while young men are bombarded hourly with anger messages about immigrants, politics, protests, white supremacy, racism, and hate.

Perspective

We live in an instant-gratification world. I want what I want, and I want it now. In this world, delaying pleasure for a greater gain is nonexistent. Adolescents expect parents to support them forever; therefore, higher education is becoming a fading pastime for many teens. They believe the world is a big fantasy island where you can do whatever you want and there are no repercussions. Life is just for fun and pleasure. The problem is in this world you can never get enough fun and pleasure and they turn to drugs, alcohol, gambling, and sex. Teenagers are exposed to pornography at the age of 9 and 10 years and develop a warped sense of what true connection and intimacy are all about.

Cultures that once shunned the outside world are now being inculcated with media, news, videos, chats, and apps, giving them access to the very debauchery they once sought to avoid. 850,000,000 messages are exchanged on an app called Discord every day, where teen videogame players can chat and set up their own private servers. An average teenager in the United States spends 280.6 minutes per month (approximately 5 hours) using Discord.

On the website Discord, kids change their names to ISIS and make 9/11 and Holocaust jokes. According to Julie Jargon of the Wall Street Journal, one mother said, "*these kids are not calling, texting or Skyping each other anymore. They're all just Discording.*" The going sentence is, "Go kill yourself." Ms. Jargon logged in to set up an account and there was no prompt for her date of birth. It took 15 minutes to find porn and Nazi memes, without specifically searching for them. The company's response, "We only act if someone complains." Allowing children to access these types of apps engenders hatred, disrespect for authority, and discord with other teenagers. Then we wonder why there are mass shootings, hate crimes, and a lack of basic communication skills toward future relationships.

On the street, in the subway, or at the gym, people are subjected to other people's private conversations. People are using phone cameras in the locker room to take selfies, while people on the exercise equipment are taking a break checking their Facebook page, while others wait to use the machine.

It's all about impulse control. Teenagers may spend too much time on their phones or play video games until all hours of the night, sleeping during school. With adults, impulsivity progresses beyond simple phone addiction to behaviors that cause relationship issues like spending money online, chatting on dating sites, and social media. People who act impulsively and emotionally want instant gratification and a quick fix. Then they often regret their actions right away and this causes shame and guilt.

Impulse Control Assessment (Saying No)

Exercise:

Do you or your children repeat any of the following behaviors repeatedly? They could be an indicator of cell phone addiction:

- Texting with friends and checking for incoming texts.   Y   N

- Listening to music and watching videos using headphones.   Y   N

- Checking email and social media accounts several times a day.   Y   N

- Playing single-player video games and interactive multi-player games.   Y   N

- Worrying about cell phone battery life and access to electrical power.   Y   N

Be honest with yourself and describe how you've become compulsively attached to technology.
_____
_____

I check my emails _____ per hour. I text _____ per hour, _____ per day.

When I get bored at work, I look at _____ for _____ hours.

I can't stop _____.

My self-esteem has taken a beating because I compare myself to people on _____.

What's the worst thing that will happen if I cut down my technology usage? _____
_____

Chapter 2

The Pro-Tech Solution

Mindfulness Focuses Us

Thich Nhat Hanh, quoting The Buddha, said, *The Past is gone, the future is out of my control. I will live and relish the present moment.*

One of the solutions to technological distractions is mindfulness; the idea of living in the present moment, focusing on today, instead of reliving the past or worrying about the future. This does not mean you cannot have dreams and goals for the future; rather, don't sit and obsessively worry about it. You can't control the future anyway, so why worry about it?

Mindfulness means concentrating on one thing at a time just for concentration's sake. Mindfulness can take many forms from meditation to just sitting and focusing on what you're doing now. What gets you in trouble is that we relive the past in our minds and worry about the future. Sometimes subconsciously, feelings we felt when younger return to haunt us, and we are triggered by the same emotions. Scientific studies of addictive behavior have shown that it is virtually impossible to relapse when you're concentrating on the present moment.

One area of mindfulness that helps people with behavioral addictions is to simply notice thoughts that enter your mind. You don't have to act on your thoughts. Just let them go and think about something else. Some days you'll have angry thoughts, shameful thoughts, or sad thoughts. The more you dwell on them, the more energy and tension they cause, and you will begin to feel restless, irritable, and discontent. The remedy is viewing yourself as an observer, like a third party looking over your shoulder and you ride the wave until it settles down and loses its power in a few minutes.

Exercise:

Find a comfortable place to sit or lie down and turn your attention to your breathing as you find a spot on the wall or in the room to focus on. As you breathe in, allow your stomach to come out, hold it, and breathe out your mouth with a deliberate "huh." Repeat as you continue to focus on the spot on the wall. When thoughts or feelings flood your mind, simply push them away and focus back on your breathing.

You have discovered that when you focus on the present moment, the need for escape into an addictive mindset is minimized greatly.

What has your experience been with living in the present moment?
During the above exercise, did you feel more or less anxious?

DOI: 10.4324/9781003453185-3

How has your fear of the future diminished based on your new understanding?
What does living in the present (today) mean to you?
What stops you from letting go of the past?
Do you worry about the future? Can you control your future?
List your goals for the future. Be specific and put a time limit on it.
(I want to lose 30 pounds in 90 days, and I will achieve that by exercising 3× per week for 45 minutes and eating a Mediterranean-style diet).
List your dreams. What's in your bucket list of things you want to achieve, places you want to visit, hobbies you want to take on, adventures you want to pursue?

Be Present in This Moment

Staying in the present moment is an antidote for distractions. Real trust in a higher power that controls the future is putting in the effort and accepting the results no matter what they are. This is not easy because the people we surround ourselves with don't fully practice this—we give lip service to things we take for granted. We shouldn't judge what we have to do personally by what we assume is going on in the minds of others.

The root of all sadness is making assumptions, assigning motives, and mind reading. Assumptions are the termites of relationships. If we are to live in the present moment, we will live a calm, serene life, accomplishing intuitively what feels right now. When we grow up with a "secure attachment" we intuitively understand how to be OK, even when life isn't OK (Table 2.1).

Exercise:

What about your partner do you take for granted? _____

_____

What are three things your partner would say that annoy him/her about you? _____

_____

Give three examples when you assumed your partner meant one thing and it turned out to be false.

1.
2.
3.

Have you ever stopped asking your partner a question because you assumed you knew the answer?   Y   N

If yes, what might happen if you were simply curious and asked for clarification, before assuming you know the answer? _____

_____

On the Attachment Style graph above, examine the second column from the left entitled "Parent Seeking Care" and identify which attachment style matches your childhood experience. Then look across the columns and see how that experience has molded you into the person you are today.

Write down what you noticed and how it makes you feel. _____

_____

_____

Exercise: *(circle your favorite distractions and create alternatives)*

Common Distractions which disturb mindfulness:

- Browsing Apps
- Texting or Emailing
- Talking on the phone
- Social Media
- TV, Newspaper, Radio
- Friends or relatives
- Video Games
- Smart Phone Notifications
- _____
- _____
- _____

Alternative Coping Skills

- Practice being mindful instead of multitasking
- Write in a journal
- Exercise
- Go for a walk
- Go shopping unless you're a "shopaholic"
- Play sports
- Meditate, yoga, tai-chi, massage
- Take up a new hobby
- Read
- Smile even when you're sad
- Finish a puzzle
- Spring clean your house
- _____
- _____

Table 2.1 Attachment Styles

Attachment style	Parent seeking care	Give care by child	Self image	Negotiate	Sexuality	Addiction
SECURE ATTACHMENT	Trusting Responds Sensitively Accepting, Cooperative Emotionally Available Comforting Validating	Positive Golden Rule Give Care Supportive	Lovable, Valuable Positive self-image Autonomy Separation will not lead to loss Independent **LOVE**	Supportive attention Share how much contact they will have together Sharing feelings and wishes Right to have differences	Intimacy grows from autonomy Mutual initiation Feels understood	Less likely to have one-night stands and infidelity
INSECURE AVOIDANT FEARFUL/ AVOIDANT	Parent uncomfortable with close body contact Rejection Avoids mother and plays with toys. Will communicate when well	Ineffective support seeking Insensitive No support Inept Late	Self-soothing Need for arousal when emotionally distressed Trouble seeking care Pulls away and avoids Distressed when separated **ABUSE**	Failure to negotiate blocks intimacy Lack of empathy Hostile Aggressive	Enjoys physical contactless Into casual sex Sex without love is pleasurable No emotional connection Avoids closeness so sex is rebuffed	One-night stands Infidelity Drugs Porn Want physical aspects of sex, not intimacy Avoids closeness
INSECURE AMBIVALENT PREOCCUPIED ANXIOUS	Sometimes loving only when parent can manage and not be preoccupied or overwhelmed Hypervigilance in child No validation	Insensitive No support Inept	Has to take on more burden just to maintain connection Runs risk of losing contact Fear, less competence Craves closeness Dependent, Inattentive **NUMB**	Lacking in mutual Negotiation Risk taker	Insatiability for closeness Sexual reticence in men Strong desire for intimacy but fear of rejection Lack of romance	Exhibitionism Voyeurism BDSM Seeks reassurance and affection

(Continued)

Table 2.1 (Continued)

Attachment style	Parent seeking care	Give care by child	Self image	Negotiate	Sexuality	Addiction
INSECURE **DISORGANIZED** **DISMISSING**	Frightening Unpredictable Flee to parent for safety Flee from parent for alarm Hostile Violent	Insensitive No support Inept	Low anxiety, high avoidance Teased for crying, laughed at tears, mocking child's distress Negative self-image Damaging self-talk **BPD	GRUDGES**	Lacking in Mutual Negotiation. Wants love and to be safe. Wants connection and to be understood Can I depend on you? Do you value me?	Fear and anxiety forming relationships. Intense loneliness but wants genuine connection. See signs of rejections where non-existent. Want tryout, reassurance and consistency	Fear and stress cause erratic behavior which drives people away

Harness Your Intuition

Intuition is about integrating our emotional mind ("right brain") with our logical mind ("left brain," tapping into our intuition or what we call a gut feeling or "wise mind"). You know you are accessing your intuition when there is no small voice telling you, "Well, *maybe you shouldn't really do that.*"

We have three parts to our mind. The logical part of our mind, the emotional part, and the wise part. When we make decisions with our emotional mind, we can make rash, impulsive, split-second decisions without thinking about the consequences. We want instant gratification and ignore what may have happened last time we gave in to our impulses. Acting impulsively leads to out-of-control behaviors, which can create chaos, destroy tryout and we end up losing our tempers, locked up in jail for a DUI, sick from an overdose or even dead. Logical mind is the part of our mind that can be reasonable and rational. People who are more logical-minded think in terms of facts, figures, cause, and effect. They can also overthink and allow the details to control them and their situation. This is important for learning skills and making more informed decisions. It is much easier when you are healthy because when you're sick, tired, lonely, or scared, your emotional mind takes over. The problem is, acting with only our logical mind leaves out the emotional element, and we need both to make intuitive decisions and both to be healthy.

For example, say a matchmaker approaches you and tells you about a person who is about the same height as you, same religion, same city, same interests. Acting on your logical mind, it seems you might want to go out with this person. However, you meet the person and there is no chemistry, you cannot stand their personality. Therefore, without emotions, deciding just based on logic is not a wise decision.

A wise decision would be to take both the logical and emotional elements and put them together; forming an intuitive gut feeling what you're deciding is the correct decision. But when a little voice pops up in your head and says, "maybe you shouldn't do this," it's a signal you're not using your wise mind or intuition.

Emotional Mind	**Rational Mind**	**Wise Mind**
		Solving the Problem
Anger		
I'm going to get even with him	That would feel good but won't solve the problem	I just have to move on and use it as a learning experience and not do it again. Getting even won't help

Focus on One Task at a Time

Focusing on one task at a time is the opposite of multitasking. It is a great skill for people whose minds are constantly racing with thoughts, feelings, worries, and anxiety. When people concentrate on one thing at a time with awareness, they focus their mind, body, effort, and attention on what they are doing in the present moment. This trains your brain not to relive the past or worry about the future. For example, when you're eating breakfast, instead of reading the newspaper, looking at the cellphone, listening to TV or radio, concentrate on what you're eating. Become aware of the smells of the fresh coffee brewing, the crunch of your cereal, the tastes and textures that make what you're experiencing unique.

To make your partner feel like a priority, instead of each of you separately texting people on your cellphone, be mindful of the person you're with, what they are saying, their body language, and their values, beliefs, and preferences.

One of the most effective ways to focus on one thing at a time is simply observing your thoughts and feelings; being mindful that you're having angry thoughts, fearful feelings, shameful thoughts, sad thoughts, and figuring out what happened before these thoughts that may be causing them. Distractions, obsessions, and compulsions cause us to numb out our feelings with technology, shopping, drugs, alcohol, sex, food, and video games. According to Brene Brown, in her TED talk on Shame and Vulnerability, *when we numb out negative feelings, thinking we will feel better or feel nothing, we're also numbing out positive feelings of joy and happiness.*

Hilary Jacobs Hendel mentions in her book, *It's Not Always Depression*, that the mere recognition of a feeling begins the process of healing. She says, *At any given moment, we can access our openhearted state by being in touch with our core emotions, instead of allowing anxiety, shame and guilt to block them.*

The Inner Self: Living in an Openhearted State of Being

What differentiates us as human beings from animals is we have a core soul that strives to live a life of calmness and serenity amidst the distractions of everyday living and the demands of our bodies. The inner self yearns for calm, curiosity, compassion, connectedness, confidence, creativity, courage, and clarity.

The reason focusing is so effective is that when a person multitasks, they add stress, doubt, and disorganized thought to the process and results suffer. Cherishing the now and making the most of each experience makes our lives more meaningful.

Some people are lucky and can spend a good part of their lives in this open-hearted state. They probably have enjoyed a secure attachment with a parent or caregiver. The rest of you struggle with trauma and insecure attachments like avoidance, dismissiveness, and preoccupation, and this causes you to distract yourself and not focus, to relieve the pain of shame, guilt, and anxiety.

Exercise: Describe a roadmap you would design to get you from where you are now to the following feelings:

- To remain Calm, I will: _____
- I am Curious about: _____
- To feel more Connected I need to: _____

- I feel Compassionate when I: _____
- I am Confident I can achieve: _____
- For me, being Courageous means: _____
- One thing I'm Clear about is: _____
- I know I'm in touch with my core emotions when: _____
- When I numb out negative emotions with substances or behaviors I'm also numbing out: _____

Appreciate What You Used to Take for Granted

In order to have gratitude for small things in our lives, it's important to be able to simply observe and describe them without being judgmental. Once you develop the skill of being able to see the good in people, it will help you become a priority by recognizing your own self-worth. Then you will be able to see the good in yourself and finally feel a sense of hope and freedom.

Exercise:

Use just the facts to describe good things you see in:

A special person in your life _____

Nature _____

The world around you _____

Describe what you know and what you see, hear, or feel, and try not to leave anything out.
_____
_____

Describe what you observe in terms of color, texture, smell, taste, or sound. _____
_____
_____

Affirmations Exercise:

Think about your own strengths and interests, what you enjoy, and how you plan on making a difference in your life and in the lives of others.

I enjoy _____ _____ _____ _____ _____ _____

I am good at (strengths) _____ _____ _____ _____ _____

I have overcome _____. The lessons I learned were _____
_____

After you fill in the blanks take each word and fit it into these questions:

I wonder how soon I will realize I am _____

How soon will I realize I am capable of _____

Why am I so _____

Why do I respect _____

Why do I accept _____

Other people may not make you a priority because your feelings are closed off, shut down, or hidden away in a safe place in your brain. When you want to become a priority, share your feelings without being judgmental, accusatory, or assuming the other person knows what you mean.

Remember, assumptions are the termites of relationships. Without assuming you know what your partner is feeling, thinking, or doing, how can you share your feelings without being judgmental, accusatory, or assuming something?

_____

_____

One way to be less judgmental, accusatory, or assuming too much is to ask more questions and repeat back what you're hearing to make sure your assumptions are correct.

What I hear you saying is _____. Is that correct?

What is causing you to bring this up all of a sudden?

I'm assuming you mean_____, is that correct?

Many people have trouble describing how they feel and simply tune out or act out obsessively to avoid putting words to their feelings. A person might say, "I'm having angry thoughts," or "I'm having sad thoughts." It's not your job to judge the thoughts, but to figure out what might be causing the anger or sadness and use another skill to reduce the emotional turmoil. The trick is that a person does not have to act on their thoughts or feelings. They are just thoughts and feelings. Instead, simply observe them, describe them non-judgmentally, and let them go from your mind, replacing them with a past, safe, positive experience.

The language we use when describing something needs to conform to reality. It's easy to confuse reality when our mind distorts it. Texting shuts out body language, intonation, and meaning. It causes people to assume what the person means without giving them the benefit of the doubt or asking for clarification. By describing a situation without judgment, a person will be able to practice getting in touch with their reality, versus the sense of isolation, boredom, and resentment that come from feeling you're not a priority in the life of a loved one.

It is also important to use positive language when describing something like your thoughts, feelings, and beliefs. Saying things like "my life is in shambles," or "I'm feeling down and depressed today," reinforces the mood and it can end up being a self-fulfilling prophecy. On the other hand, when a person speaks positively, it gives them a sense of hope and inspiration.

Appreciation Exercise:

Gratitude benefits the relationship and is a result of appreciation. Appreciation affects your soul and does not require action. When we appreciate someone, we feel seen and valued, as though we belong. Unfortunately for many of you, appreciation does not fit with how we learned to communicate with family and with others. Some of you grew up expecting pain, distrust, anger, resentment, and bitterness instead of joy. We learned to be critical of others instead of being understanding and giving people the benefit of the doubt.

We expect the worst, and we become critical. Instead of being tender toward weakness, we criticize the people around us. Our past experiences foster rejection, depression, overwhelm, and despair. When we grow up with a negative glass-half-empty attitude, we overlook memories of God's goodness. When we can begin to notice and appreciate the goodness He bestows upon us, we strengthen our minds to begin habitually noticing the good in the environment around us. We have gratitude.

Sharing gratitude is a simple way to intentionally communicate positively as a couple. This practice can strengthen the bond between you and deepen the soulful knowledge of one another. A couple sharing in this practice can strengthen their bond, increase positive interactions, and help each other to see the other through God's eyes.

Make a list of 25 things you are grateful for:

_____   _____   _____
_____   _____   _____
_____   _____   _____
_____   _____   _____
_____   _____   _____
_____   _____   _____
_____   _____   _____

Form them into Cheerleading Statements for daily review.

(I have gratitude for _____)
(I appreciate _____ about my _____ .

_____ _____ _____
_____ _____ _____
_____ _____ _____
_____ _____ _____
_____ _____ _____
_____ _____ _____
_____ _____ _____
_____ _____ _____

What are you thankful for today? _____

What makes you smile? _____

What do you notice when you express appreciation? Appreciation is packaged joy. _____
_____

Identify three qualities you appreciate about another person. _____
_____

Judge People Favorably, Including Yourself

It is impossible not to judge on some level. It's a lot like gossip. A person knows they will probably gossip and say something negative or derogatory this coming year. Yet, when he observes his thoughts, he can ask himself, "Does this person really need to know this bit of juicy gossip?" Probably not. The same is true with judging ourselves and others. We have a choice to judge or not to judge and it all depends on remaining aware of the classic dialectical question: "What helps me move closer to a life worth living?"

Let go of what is right or wrong, should of, could haves, and comparing ourselves to others. Judging and comparing are a person's worst enemies. None of you are perfect creatures, and we all make mistakes. Give yourself a break and stop trying to be perfect in your eyes and in the eyes of others. When a person can express who they really are, they will find a way to be kind, understand, and committed to a life worth living. This quest is what emotional freedom is all about. Just because we are not abusing drugs or alcohol, sleeping around, or gambling does not mean we are emotionally sober. Being nonjudgmental of ourselves and others is one key to unlock the mystery of working toward a prioritized life worth living.

Exercise:

What would you do if you didn't have to do it perfectly? _____
_____

Whose expectations are you trying to meet? _____
_____

Proverbs 24:16 states, *A righteous person falls seven times and gets up* You would think a person who falls seven times would be a wicked person. It's coming to teach you that the definition of a righteous person is someone who keeps getting up after falling many times. A wicked person would be someone who falls, keeps falling, and never gets up. If this is the case, there is no reason to judge others because there is a possibility they may have needed to fall to understand how to get up; and when they make the effort to improve and get up, even seven times, they are considered righteous, so how can we judge them?

Share Your Story Exercise:

List two examples of times you've gotten up after falling and what you remember. What was the lesson you learned from this experience?

_____

_____

_____

Play by the Rules: What Is Real Freedom?

Freedom from modern-day obsessions and compulsions does not mean we are free to do as we please without facing consequences. Psychologists view freedom from the perspective that people are motivated by pleasure, according to Freud, and by power, according to Adler. Victor Frankl posits that human beings strive to find meaning in their lives. This is a synthesis of all three into one model, according to David Lieberman, PhD, in *How Free Will Works*. He says, t*he pursuit of meaning gives you maximum pleasure, the prerequisite of which is self-regulation, which is the highest form of power: the ability to maintain control over oneself.*

Becoming an effective communicator is all about doing what works, playing by the rules, letting go of vengeance, anger, and who is right or wrong. It comfortably accents the idea of recognizing the polka dots of life, opportunities for growth without judgment, giving people the benefit of the doubt, and not holding on to old resentments, jealousy, and revenge. When we can do this successfully, we can easily make loved ones a priority without sacrificing ourselves.

To be effective in life, one must know what his goals are. Not having a goal in life is like walking in a forest without a map. You have no idea where you're going, how to reach your destination, and how to get out of danger. When a person has a goal, they have something to look forward to achieving and this becomes the impetus to move forward, despite the odds, to accomplish something in life.

When you accept a situation, you are being more effective. People are naturally more effective when they stop saying things should be this way or that way. It means playing by the rules even when you don't think they are fair. Without rules, our lives would be chaotic. Playing by the rules helps bring order and mindfulness into our lives, so we can accomplish our goals and be as effective as possible. It doesn't hinder our freedom; instead, it creates an opportunity to find order and symmetry in our lives.

Imagine a story where Joe is told there is a buried treasure in a city park. Joe begins to look around and suddenly a wise old man, Jacob comes over to Joe and tells him he has the map to where the buried treasure is. Joe says, "I don't want to be enslaved to your map to find this treasure, I am free to look wherever I want to find the treasure." That's stupidity, not freedom. A map or blueprint for living our lives is the true freedom from the distractions around us.

Being effective also means letting go of trying to get even with someone who has hurt you. It is a natural reaction to want to get even, but hardly effective in creating a meaningful relationship. Instead, learn to give people the benefit of the doubt; try to understand the situation from their point of view. If your anger is justified, express it without rage. Or, let go of the anger of who is right or wrong and focus on an effective solution. Many times, our anger is not justified, and we let what others are doing or saying disturb our peace of mind. Being effective is letting go of extremes and focusing on the compromise position or mutual benefit. Passivity is not necessarily passive. Letting go is a choice.

Exercise: The Four Styles of Communication

1. **Passive:** Passive is a style where individuals avoid expressing their feelings, protecting their own rights and identifying and meeting their own needs. Therefore, passive individuals do not respond to hurtful or anger-producing situations. Instead, they hold on to the resentment and allow several resentments to build up before they finally lash out with explosive outbursts. After the outburst, they realize their reaction was out of proportion to the current situation and they feel guilt, shame, remorse, and confusion.
2. **Aggressive:** Aggressive is a style where individuals express their needs, opinions, and beliefs in a way that   violates the rights of others. Aggressive communicators are either physically or verbally abusive.
3. **Passive Aggressive:** Passive aggressive individuals appear passive on the surface but are actually acting out in anger in a subtle, indirect, or behind-the-scenes way. They usually feel powerless, stuck, and resentful and tend to undermine the object of their resentment through sarcasm, denial, and mismatched facial expressions.
4. **Assertive:** Assertive people clearly state their opinions and feelings and firmly advocate for their rights and beliefs without violating the rights of others. They value themselves, their time, and their emotional needs while being respectful of others.

The Story of the Check-out Line in a Supermarket

Imagine you're standing in the checkout line at the supermarket, and someone breaks in line in front of you. You now have four choices on how you will respond.

- You can physically push the guy out of the line (aggressive).
- You can let him break line without saying anything (passive).
- You can let him break line, say nothing, go home, and complain about what they did (passive aggressive).
- Or, you can say, *You broke line, please go to the back of the line*

Give examples in the box to the right of each way you communicate

Communication style	Your examples
Aggressive	
Passive	
Passive Aggressive	
Assertive	

Exercise:

To me, freedom means...

*What gives my life meaning is*_____

In my addiction I think I have the freedom to do as I please, but in reality _____

_____

If I forgive it means I am _____

If I accept a situation or person, it means I _____

*Rules, boundaries, and laws are necessary because*_____

_____

Goal Setting: The Angle of Hope and Freedom

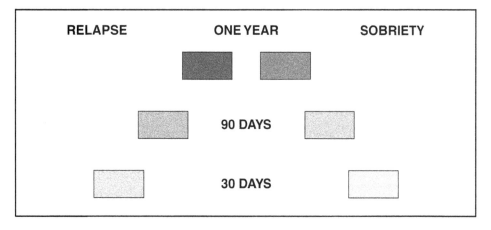

Illustration: Angle of opportunity

Fighting versus Letting Go

We can use mindfulness of our emotions to push away irrational thoughts.

It's not your body you have to control, it's your mind. Switch your thinking and your body will heal. You can only have one thought in your mind at a time. Use your mind for a change!!!!! The key to emotional freedom is to live in the moment, just for today, just for the hour, just for the minute. Stop reliving your past, it's over and you can't change it. Stop worrying about the future. You are not in control.

The more you fight to be in control of everything around you, the more you'll fall and keep stumbling. Let go, relax, and let your Higher Power control things for you. Accept what is happening to you is what your Higher Power wants to happen. HE will help you but you have to be willing to accept HIM being in control. You have to become a pure accepting vessel before your Higher Power will fill you up with serenity.

Addiction is not about the substance or behavior. It's that we use these behaviors to cover up a spiritual hole yearning for connection and intimacy with another person. It pushes people you love away from you, who want you to make them a priority. Instead, we're stuck on our phones and computers, afraid to be vulnerable enough to share our emotions, hopes, and dreams with the person we're sharing our lives with.

Exercise:

Draw an image in each box that represents the life you hope to have moving forward.

PASSION   MEANING   PURPOSE   INTEGRITY   FREEDOM
HOPE

Mindfulness Exercise:

Close your eyes and use your imagination to create positive, healthy images of places you've been where you've felt a sense of serenity, peace of mind, and happiness. Use all your senses, see the sights, hear the sounds, feel the feelings you once felt and relive this experience in your mind. This works because our subconscious mind does not know the difference if we're at home or at the beach when we can visualize this type of happy or safe place. Go ahead, close your eyes, and do it now.

What gives your life meaning? _____

What are you passionate about? _____

Create a short-term goal for yourself to find meaning and passion. _____

Prayer can be a mindfulness experience by itself. Look in Psalms and find one that resonates with your situation and life experiences and then offers hope for the future. The author of Psalms,

King David, was a praying man. He was also someone who struggled in life, with temptations, enemies, and many battles. But his prayers of gratitude (Psalms) were his path to peace and are still recited to this day.

Do something for yourself for a change, making yourself a priority. Take a stroll in the park, get a healthy massage, meditate, take a nap. Do something every day to make your life less stressful. _____

Be mindful of one problem at a time. Don't try and swallow the entire elephant all at once. Take a crisis you're in now and deal with it, accept it, or change it.

Meditation Practice

You may want to record this meditation so you can relax.

Begin with some simple breathing, noticing the coolness of your breath as you breathe in and the warmth of the breath as you breathe out. Imagine a soft, white cloud entering your brain, and moving down the body, limb by limb, organ by organ, loosening the tightness, smoothing out the muscles and tendons, and relaxing.

I wonder how quickly and easily you will become aware of how mindful you can truly become… to concentrate on your breathe, and in the unlikely event your mind drifts away into the past or into the future, how easily you bring it back into focus in your mind's eye as you continue to concentrate on your breathing… I want you to STOP and consider enjoying this new feeling of calmness as you listen to my voice guide you… so that now and in the future you can remain mindful of what is going on around you and bring your feelings and emotions into your awareness easily and naturally…. and when you do you might notice how naturally and easily one might experience unlimited pleasure. Have you ever imagined what your life would be like if you could naturally use these skills when your feelings were less than perfect? Naturally, I am sure you are aware that this experience can bring you un-limited amounts of joy and excitement beyond what you could ever imagine yourself as you move beyond any limitations and begin to expand your skills until they delight you, using them to easily reach your full potential, make new healthy choices and connections… and in the days, weeks, and months ahead become mindful—STOP—Get a hold of yourself—and remember, the memory may not STOP the hurt BUT it can START the healing. When you say to yourself, I wonder how free I will be when I let go of resentments? How delighted will I be when I realize I have a choice to be RIGHT or to be HAPPY and I choose to be Happy.

Begin to realize that most people fail to realize that their feelings toward others are determined by their feelings toward themselves and there is no reason to be afraid of storms because you are learning through these skills how to sail your own ship riding the waves of your emotions until they simply and easily fade away into the wind.

And now, you might want to imagine walking up a stairway, and with every step up you be-come a little more awake, a little more aware of the energy in this room surrounded by the other group members. When I count to 10, you can simply open your eyes and come back into the room. 1-2-3 beginning to wiggle your fingers and toes; 4-5-6 beginning to feel a sense of being awake and present; 7-8 being mindful of the energy in the room, feeling willing and alive; 9-10 you can open your eyes and come back into the room.

Tele Exercise:

After you have *listened* to the guided meditation above, sit quietly for five minutes, close your eyes and just notice what feelings and thoughts come up. Journal about what you noticed.

_____

_____

_____

_____

Technology Addiction Exercise:

List ten ways being glued to technology has made your life unmanageable.

_____

_____

_____

_____

_____

_____

_____

_____

_____

_____

Ten consequences of your actions toward your family, work, money, self.

_____

_____

_____

_____

_____

_____

_____

_____

_____

_____

Trace back what is happening in other parts of your life that are making you fearful, angry, lonely, tired, anxious, or bored.

What is the payoff for you to keep acting out? (There is always a benefit, or you wouldn't be doing it).

_____

_____

How can you make your partner the priority in your life from now on without giving up on yourself?

_____

_____

We will continue to struggle with technology, and these powerful distractions will continue to haunt us until we put them down, take a technology holiday, and discover we can live without it, even for one day.

Section II

Work

Chapter 3

Subjected to the Daily Grind

Work Defines Us: I Am a Human Doing Rather Than a Human Being

If I were to ask you, "What do you do?" You would probably answer what type of work you do to earn a living. You're defining yourself by the work you do. What about how you volunteer for non-profit organizations, give charity, invite friends over for dinner, or the fact that you were once the National President of a Youth Organization at the age of 18? Why do we define ourselves by the work we do instead of being the person we really are—a human being?

We become addicted to work, thinking we have to get all the work done today and spend endless hours at the office, making work our priority instead of our wife and kids. Even when we're home, we're constantly checking our emails or accepting calls, texts, and emails from our boss at 11 p.m. because we allow them to think we're available 24/7.

Within every industry, there are experts who are willing to teach you how to become successful for a fee. "If I would only invest another $5,000.00 in just one more marketing system, all my financial problems would be over and my life would be changed forever. Then, when you invest the money, you're given bits and pieces of information until you spend another $15,000.00 to meet the guru himself, who will deliver the real secret to your success. It's an intoxicating game of roulette, making you think we don't know enough to make a success of ourselves and we become enslaved to the opportunity to make more money, without considering what we are really sacrificing to get there.

On one hand, work can be addictive in a good sense. Entrepreneurs, for example, need passion, enthusiasm, and a drive to succeed. On the other hand, when passion, money, fortune, and fame drive you toward being a slave to work, it begins to affect other areas of our lives negatively, and we lose control. Doubt sets in as we question our own ability to work at what we're passionate about. Fear of success and fear of failure get in the way, flooding our decision-making consciousness, and we begin to crave distractions to numb the pain of self-doubt and fear.

Work, rest, play, read, write, enjoy, savor, sensual, exercise, music, whatever feels right…. right now. And it doesn't have to be good feelings only, like eating or playing. If we choose work that is meaningful and fun, our lives can be transformed from myopic drudgery to ecstatic rejuvenation. Simply from a switch of priorities…from a shift from what others expect of me to what I

DOI: 10.4324/9781003453185-5

This question is often asked in 12-step meetings. Are you a human doing or a human being?

Human doing	*vs.*	*Human being*

feel I want to do now. The challenge is money. Ask yourself, "what is my passion and how can I turn that passion into a conduit for earning a living?

Values Exercise

John Green says, "*I just want to do something that matters. Or be something that matters. I just want to matter.*"

What do you value? (Family, personal, exercise, money, faith, work, integrity, honesty, emotional health, etc.) _____

How will you feel when you finally realize your dreams? _____

What will you do specifically to realize your dreams? _____

When do you remember feeling failure for the first time? _____

When do you remember feeling success for the first time? _____

I am spending most of my time _____

To reach my goals, I need to allocate my time differently to find balance in my life. I will achieve this by _____

I can make better choices by _____

I want the world to see me as _____

I really am in the world (my identity, what gives my life meaning)

_____

Where do I find meaning in life? (Work, children, partner, religion, heritage, money, power, prestige, music, hobbies, etc.) _____

How can I connect better to others? (the world, the universe, my community, my relationships)
_____ _____ _____

What parts of yourself have you discarded and disowned? (*I don't/won't* dance, sing, cry, get angry, draw, love, be prejudiced, hate) _____ _____
_____ _____

When I am "being" and not "doing" I feel passionate about? _____

A metaphor for my life would be? (Roller coaster, skydiving, stuck in the mud, merry-go-round...)
_____

My inner compass points to the cup being Half Full or Half Empty _____

When I am simply being present with someone I feel _____

Say a Little Prayer for Yourself and Write It Down

Write a prayer that speaks to your own personal values. Here's an example:

God, you have given me so much abundance: A wife who loves me unconditionally, a successful practice, relatively good health, intelligence, compassion, and empathy. May I learn to have compassion and empathy toward myself? I tryout that You reward those who tryout in You and pray every day for clarity and vision to do the next right thing that will bring honor to You, letting go of self-seeking and focusing on what I can do to serve You, rather than looking to others to validate me by doing what I think is the right way. Grant me the serenity to understand my power comes from doing the next right thing, on my watch, without judging or comparing what I do, believe, or expect from others. Power is standing up for myself to be who I am openly, to treat myself with respect in all human and person encounters. Help me to understand how to accept things I cannot change while giving me the wisdom to speak up for myself and what I believe; to exact change in the world and in my community, but not at the expense of holding on to resentments, anger, or irritability. I am responsible for the achievement of my desires, my choices, and my actions (integrity), and I ask YOU to help me focus on what is right to serve your will and live by the Values You have set forth in the spiritual writings. And in this way I will be able to live a life of mindfulness, purpose, and integrity through enhanced self-esteem.

Seeking Fame, Respect, Success, and Honor

According to Abraham Amsel in Judaism and Psychology (1997), *The roots of mental illness are to be sought not in guilt but in gross, untamed ambitions and in gross fear of being frustrated. Neurosis arises from discontent with one's lot, which, in turn, stems from uncontrolled ambition, not guilt. Arrogance, jealousy, lust, status-seeking, fear, lack of trust are the propellants of mental illness.*

Ethics of the Fathers states that *"jealousy, lust, and honor put man out of this world."* Social psychologists Alfred Adler and Karen Horney believe that man's striving for superiority can be seen as an inclination toward arrogance as opposed to learning to be humbler.

Mitch Axelrod says in *Addictive Entrepreneurship, When you know yourself you can succeed at work. If you know everything else, but don't know yourself, you may become successful, but you won't feel fulfilled. Success without fulfillment leaves you feeling empty.*

Many people select jobs because it's the first one that hires them. To feel fulfilled, a person has to have both interest and the skills to get the job done. They have to feel they can make a difference in the lives of their clients or customers.

A client wrote, *My addiction to work and love was a vain attempt to look toward the future and focus my energy on future and potential hype instead of living and appreciating today with all its pleasures of just being alive and counting my blessings. For this I have missed living a full life of appreciating what I have and my own unique strengths.*

Instead, we miss living true to ourselves by escaping into fantasy, attracted to outlandish get-rich-quick claims, hype and the promises of a bright future. We have missed being ourselves by being busy waiting for others to tell you how to be somebody, instead of relying on our own intuition.

Exercise:

Write two sentences about how you escape into fantasy:

    1. _____
    2. _____
    3. **When do you escape into fantasy?** _____
    4. **What is the feeling that precipitates the escape?** _____

How do you reconcile living in the present moment with needing to have goals, dreams, and aspirations for your future? _____

How can a person be happy if he is satisfied with what he has, rather than spending a fortune to learn how to make a fortune? _____

How do you know you truly know yourself? _____

If you do not know yourself, what is missing? _____

Are you coexisting in your relationship or being yourself? (open, vulnerable, integrity, honesty) _____

List five things you know about yourself: (I am….)

    1. _____
    2. _____
    3. _____
    4. _____

We do not enjoy what we have because we're always searching for new possibilities. Living in the present is our challenge.
Write two sentences about what <u>you</u> are searching for:

_____

_____

Expectations Are Premeditated Resentments

According to Al-Anon's *Courage to Change*, Expectations are premeditated resentments.

When a person expects another person to act a certain way, he is usually disappointed. From early childhood, we experience spoken or unspoken rules that feed our expectations. When a child gets 4 As and 1 B on a report card and the parent focuses on why the child got a B, it sets up the child to be a perfectionist. Later in life, the need to be perfect permeates our essence, and we're forever expecting everything we do to meet past expectations of perfectionism.

We cannot expect other people to make you happy or do our work for you. We have to work and do the best we can within our capabilities, strengths, and interests. The problem is "shoulds" haunt you like a gnawing dragon gripping our sore shoulders. "I should be working on this project but I'm stuck stuffing envelopes for the non-profit I reluctantly volunteered to help. I should be writing a proposal for a new client, but what if it's not good enough or not perfect?" "Shoulds become our inner critic. We compile to-do lists and then spend hours deciding whether to write them down on paper or add them to the fourth email organizer I just downloaded. After all, I only check my email every 10 minutes or less. This way I can have my email or an app remind me every second of the day what I "should" be doing.

Addiction protects my pain of expectations. That's why resentment is the worst enemy of the addict. People expect things to be a certain way and when they don't turn out that way, they protect themselves by acting out. As a client wrote, *"the isolation and loneliness I feel, those walls I construct to keep people out, this struggle to connect and push away at the same time, makes me want to connect but I equate connection with love."*

Exercise:

If my work is not perfect, it means _____

As a child, I could have used a lot more _____

But what I got growing up was _____

For years, I've often wondered about _____

Shame frame:	Dispute the belief
I should _____	_____
I must_____	_____
I'm always _____	_____
I'm never _____	_____

Using Work to Avoid Problems at Home

Work suffers when there are arguments and discord at home. When there is infidelity, for example, the betrayer becomes enslaved to the fear of going home and facing yet another barrage of questions and nasty comments about his past actions. Some people use the excuse; they have so much work to do but spend four hours a day drinking coffee, playing video games, and making small talk around the water fountain.

Even in healthy relationships, stress at work can affect one's personal life. When one partner wants to share the stresses of her day and the other is not in the mood to listen and support her, it causes friction and a feeling of "what about supporting me in my time of need?" The rules are clear.

Conflicting work schedules also create discord. When one person works the day shift and one the night shift, they never have time except on the weekends to spend time together. There is an obligatory salute of "have a nice day," as you go to sleep and your wife goes to work. Couples find that when one partner quits a stressful job that creeps into the weekends, they are much calmer, happier, and healthier, even if they make less money. A person has to decide what his priorities are. The choices are to live a serene, calm family life or experience stress and health issues caused by always working.

How Work Deprives Us of Our Freedom: A Case Study

People who work don't enjoy it or feel fulfilled and avoid their passion, even temporarily.

A client wrote a letter to his "addict" about how it prevents him from succeeding.

Dear Addiction,

Why do you continually threaten my sanity? Isn't it enough for the past 57 years you have destroyed my ambition? You've convinced me to turn aside my good qualities and strengths and focus on destructive distractions that will kill me spiritually and physically. Leave me alone and let me understand the difference between when play is appropriate and when more work is. Why must you cover me in your blanket of shame and guilt further alienating me from my spirit? Is it because you don't believe I'll ever be good enough? Or just to punish me more than I already feel.

I sometimes feel like crying in mourning because of what you've done to me; convincing me I'm a hypocrite and not letting me accept the slow pace of the healing process. Leave me alone and let me live a few years of peace and serenity where I can go forward with my strengths and live in the present moment. I can still be a good person even if I slip up while recovering. But you insist on perfection and compare me to all the successes of extended sobriety. I don't want to have these drunken feelings of hangover any longer, so stop pestering me to give in. I have too much time to accomplish more, but just as fear of success rears its ugly head, I jeopardize myself out of deference to you.

What is my ultimate payoff? I feel entitled to escape the resentments for things not working out as others promised they would. Lowering expectations is like under promising and over delivering. But you've convinced me that fear is my friend and instead of action, you put fear in its stead to tempt me into feeling entitled to screw up. Well, I'm tired of screwing up.

What is it that pulls me to waste time and not get important work done? What is the payoff of constantly bombarding me with temptation to mess up? Can't you see I have latent talents hidden in the recesses of my brain hoping to be recognized for their generosity in educating people for nothing? When are you going to allow me to break away and demand I get paid what I'm worth? It's time! Time is running out. Money is running out. Hope springs eternal. Fragments of hope bristle in my face, but you've prevented me from enjoying them. Anxiety racks my body with shock waves because you're always in the driver's seat. Get out of my car and let me drive.

The wisdom to know the difference is my biggest challenge. Standing in the middle of life, not knowing, not caring, which way to turn. You've numbed my sense of balance. Yet, I know my gut will tell me what I need to believe. Gut-wrenching boundaries are my only defense against you. Yet, you insist on jumping over the fence. When will you release me and let me enjoy a few moments of serenity? In the grave perhaps? Not in this hell on earth. Not when you're still on the loose unbridled by lust, red by resentment, fired up by anger, kindled with fear. I can only escape you when I live in the present moment. Yet you lurk in the darkest corners in the recesses of my mind, taunting me. Stop It! Your claws grab me by the neck and squeeze rational thinking out of my brain onto the floor below, to wallow in the filth of escapism. Escape is my only solace when you grip me. Then I cannot, I will not stop until you consume me and I am at the bottom of the dung heap, climbing out once again to meet the next challenge you throw my way.

Exercise:

How do you use work to avoid going home and being with family? _____

How much money is going to be enough? _____

Can you be happy with less money and a more fulfilling life? _____

How do your expectations lead to resentments? _____

What is your motivation for seeking fame, fortune, success, and honor? _____
_____

How will you lessen your workload to spend more time with your family? _____
_____

How much time do you allocate for fun each week? _____

What is the payoff for working such long hours? _____

Could I work less, charge more, and make the same amount of money, and have time to do something fun for myself? _____

Write a letter about your addiction to work using the above example as a reference by putting yourself in the shoes of members of your family.

_____

_____

_____

_____

_____

_____

_____

TIME BLOCKING CHART

Time	Sunday	Monday	Tuesday	Wednesday	Thursday	Friday	Saturday

Consider the following activities and place them in the box along with the time period. For example, Sunday 3–5 Football. Include TV, Internet, Sleeping, Eating, Working, Playing, Family, Other.

Chapter 4

Fun in the Sun Protector

Play and Rest Strengthen Us

Healthy human beings nurture themselves with friends, hobbies, games, rest, exercise, and self-care.

Work/Life Balance

Some people are so poor, they only have their money.

Tami Forman is Executive Director of PathForward.org, a nonprofit organization on a mission to empower people to restart their careers after time spent focused on caregiving. She says,

> If I've learned anything, since I became a working mom, it is that there isn't a "right" way to have work/life balance. Knowing what will bring you the balance you seek requires you to know what makes you feel balanced! What gives you energy and what drains you? How many hours can you work before you feel your productivity start to slip? Do you have times of the day when you are more productive and times when you are less productive? How much sleep and exercise do you need? What kind of diet do you need to maintain to maximize your energy?

Exercise:

What makes you feel balanced between work and play? _____

What gives you energy and what drains you? _____

How many hours can you work before you feel your productivity start to slip? _____

What are the times of the day when you are more productive and times when you are less productive?

_____

How much sleep and exercise do you need? _____

What kind of diet do you need to maintain to maximize your energy? _____

_____

DOI: 10.4324/9781003453185-6

Self-Care

Self-care is sometimes thought of as a backward concept as an indulgence. This means self-care is something we are occasionally allowed to indulge in, and it should feel like an indulgence.

(Think expensive bath products, luxurious chocolates, spa appointments). When we spend more time talking about the self-care power of fluffy down pillows than we do about getting enough sleep, we've wandered far from anything that can be remotely considered healthy for either mind or body.

Self-care is not an indulgence; it is a discipline. It requires tough-mindedness, a deep and personal understanding of your priorities, and respect for both you and the people you choose to spend your life with.

For example, self-care is one way to make yourself or your partner a priority.

Turn off the TV instead of watching another episode of "The Walking Dead" until 2 a.m. because the alarm is going off at 5 a.m. so you can get to the gym. And while you're at it, turn off the notifications on your devices and only check them twice a day. Find a reliable news source, if you can, and periodically stay in touch. Say no to the things you don't want to do, even if it will make someone upset. Find work that brings you a sense of fulfillment and purpose, instead of simply accepting the first menial job that comes along.

It takes discipline to do the things that are good for you instead of what feels good at the moment. It takes even more discipline to refuse to take responsibility for other people's emotional well-being. And it takes discipline to take full and complete responsibility for our own well-being.

Self-care is also not something you do once in a while when the world gets crazy. It's what you do every day, every week, month in and month out. It's taking care of yourself in a way that doesn't require you to "indulge" in order to restore balance. It's making the commitment to stay healthy and balanced as a regular practice.

Self-Care Challenge

List three things you can do in each category for self-care:

Physical	Emotional

Spiritual	Sexual

Finding Your Passion in Life

If your work requires so much of you that you're ignoring your wife and family, you may want to re-evaluate your purpose and passion. Understand what you want out of life, not just in business but also in relationships, spirituality, health, self-help, play, and education. It's OK for a 25-year-old to burn the midnight oil when she is just getting started in her career, but it's not a plan for the rest of your life.

Some people are trapped into working six days. Explore the alternative and find something else. What else is possible? What are your values? How does that match up with your current situation? When your job is sucking the life out of you, maybe that means it's time to look for a new house or a new job.

Don't give up your life for work. There are so many online resources you can tap into to find other alternatives. Decide what's important to you? What could you do differently? Consider whether it matches your values, goals, dreams, and purpose.

JoAnna Brandi, Certified Chief Happiness Officer at http://ReturnOnHappiness.com explains the work/life balance as energy gains and energy drains. She tells client to chart activities during the day like a call with a client, writing a new proposal, contacting her new boyfriend, et al. On a scale of 1–5 add up the drains vs. gains. Explore what can you add, subtract, or change about how you spend your time and energy.

After all, you have a choice: Change it, fix it, accept it, or stay miserable. I have a client who works for a large distribution company. They will be closing their doors in two years and have cut back their workforce. They are now shorthanded and my client has to work six days a week, with no time off on Saturdays to be with her family. Employers don't care if she can't see her grandkids, they want production quotas no matter what even if it means overtime. The problem is clients become disgruntled, go on temporary leave to reduce stress and end up in my office.

The process puts you in alignment. If she accepts her job as is, she may be in alignment. But the best alternative is to accept and reframe the situation (I'll do it for the next year, with joy, and bless my work for now. I will be kind, helpful, and willing for it to change. I will find an exit plan).

Play by the Rules

Hope and Freedom[1] do not mean that we are free to do as we please without facing consequences. Psychologists view freedom from the perspective that people are motivated by pleasure, according to Freud, and by power, according to Adler. Victor Frankl posits that human beings strive to find meaning in their lives. Judaism views this as a synthesis of all three into one model, according to Dovid Lieberman, Ph.D. in *How Free Will Works*. He says, "*the pursuit of meaning gives you maximum pleasure, the prerequisite of which is self-regulation, which is the highest form of power: the ability to maintain control over oneself.*"

Becoming an effective communicator is all about doing what works, playing by the rules, letting go of vengeance, anger, and who is right or wrong. It comfortably accents the idea of recognizing the polka dots of life, opportunities for growth without judgment, giving people the benefit of the doubt and not holding on to old resentments, jealousy, and revenge. When we can do this successfully, we can easily make loved ones a priority without sacrificing ourselves.

To be effective in life, one must know what their goals are. Not having a goal in life is like walking in a forest without a map. You have no idea where you're going, how to reach your destination, and how to get out of danger. When a person has a goal, they have something to look forward to achieving and this becomes the impetus to move forward, despite the odds, to accomplish something in life.

When you accept a situation, you are being more effective. People are naturally more effective when they stop saying things should be this way or that way. It means playing by the rules even when you don't think they are fair. Without rules, our lives would be chaotic. Playing by the rules helps bring order and mindfulness into our lives, so we can accomplish our goals and be as effective as possible. It doesn't hinder our freedom; instead, it creates opportunity to find order and symmetry in our lives.

Imagine a story where a person is told there is a buried treasure in a city park. Joe begins to look around and suddenly a wise old man, Jacob comes over to him and tells him he has the map to where the buried treasure is. Joe says, "I don't want to be enslaved to your map to find this treasure, I am free to look wherever I want to find the treasure." That's stupidity, not freedom. A map or blueprint for living our life is the true freedom from the enslavement of the distractions of self and those around us.

Being effective also means letting go of trying to get even with someone who has hurt you. It is a natural reaction to want to get even, but hardly effective in creating a meaningful relationship. Instead, learn to give people the benefit of the doubt; try to understand the situation from their point of view. If your anger is justified, express it without rage. Or, let go of the anger of who is right or wrong and focus on an effective solution. Many times, our anger is not justified and we let what others are doing or saying disturb our peace of mind. Being effective is letting go of extremes and focusing on the compromise position or mutual benefit.

Finding a work/life rhythm. Why play is so important to re-energize yourself?
Any activity for human connection is what is needed in place of technology.
Here are a few ideas to find a work/life rhythm and balance:
Come up with one idea in each category that you can begin

- Singing builds vagal tone. So does gargling, humming, and chanting. They all increase vagal tone and happiness.
  I will _____ for 5 minutes every day at _____ a.m./p.m.

- Getting together with friends, joining a support group, or creating a process where people check in and process bragging and attitude. People in the group ask: What happened to you the week before—brag about it. Affirm the positive. Each person expresses gratitude and the group acknowledges it.
  I will join a _____ group within 14 days and I will express gratitude to _ _____ for _____.

- Adult play group—willing to do fun things together,
  Healthy, fun things I plan to do are _____

- Celebration of significant events.
  I will celebrate significant events in my life by _____

- If you don't know how to play—go find children, even sick children, meet up and make their day fun.

- Go to an art studio, bake cupcakes, take a long walk or a short nap.
  What I plan to do for fun for myself in the coming week is _____

_____

Play

You can combine play with exercise. Play physically discharges energy.
People who are enslaved to work, spending, sex, food, need help in finding play.
What gets you going? _____
What kind of hobbies did you have as a kid? _____
You need to get lost in yourself and in the flow to find play.
Did you ever consider swimming, stamp collecting, hiking, or skydiving? Which?

_____

Exercise:

How do you escape the pressures of your life? _____
What makes you curious and excited about life? _____
Who can you teach what you know?_____

Being an instructor is relational and will replace loneliness and isolation. Many people need an adrenaline rush and use process addictions to soothe themselves. Find something more moderate to get adrenaline-based.

Prevention

All of you are vulnerable to triggers from time to time that cause you to crave and have urges for quick fix relief from emotional turmoil. Many people become more vulnerable when they are hungry, angry, lonely, or tired. When a person is in this frame of mind, his senses are dulled, and his decision-making capabilities are altered. Then restless, irritable and discontent feelings follow, sometimes over a period of hours, days, even weeks, or months and we are on our way toward relapse.

Stay focused on positive feelings and behaviors, and don't slip into hunger, anger, loneliness, or being tired. It is the actions we take daily to make our lives worth living and give us the emotional rest we need to prosper.

A Day of Rest—Sabbath[2]

The 23rd Psalm by King David says, *"He makes me lie down in green pastures; He leads me beside still waters; He restores my soul."*

The idea of a day of rest is to help restore you from the stresses, trials, and tribulations of the workweek. A gift of time where we allow the work in the marketplace to disappear so we can focus on spirituality. We set aside time to relish being alive, to celebrate happiness and freedom with family and friends, to learn to appreciate natural things we take for granted and give thanks for the very act of being on top of the ground instead of below it. Yes, it's another archaic idea from the Bible, but don't knock it until you've tried it. Just set aside your cellphone for a day and you'll experience a sense of wonder, peace, and tranquility of not having to constantly be on call.

Sabbath is an active state of being rather than a passive state of doing nothing. Our purpose in this world is to work, but when work becomes all-encompassing, it is time for rest. A day of rest to experience reality, stepping back, and spiritually evaluating our lives, our purpose, and our mission in life. Without rest, we're like mice on a perpetually moving wheel, filling our lives for the accumulation of fortune and fame, without allowing ourselves to respite (one day a week) from the daily grind.

When we work seven days a week, we become a human doing instead of a human being. In kindling the light of a day of rest, we affirm ourselves and the world around us, the importance of being rather than doing.

We can sense when it is time to relax. If we had a heart attack, we would have no choice but to rest and relax. So, make rest and relaxation a priority and you'll reap the benefits of more productivity at work and a more balanced lifestyle.

Take the 24-hour Sabbath Challenge (Many People of Faith Practice This Every Week! You Can Do It)?

Select a 24-hour period where you will not work at the office or at home, no chores, no numbing out with your cell phone, movies, news, or TV. Disengage from the world around you and focus on your family and yourself, eating together, praying together, and talking about important issues that affect your family, your community, and the world around you.

Write below about what you noticed after your 24-hour Sabbath Challenge

_____

_____

_____

_____

The Freedom of Happiness

We seek happiness through spectator sports, hobbies, technological objects, the Internet, food, shopping, glamorous movie stars, entertainment, personal trainers, vintage wine, and coffee (The Best Part of Waking Up is Folgers in your Cup).

True happiness comes when we become givers not takers, when we give of ourselves to help others including our spouses and family. Linking happiness to fulfilling every life pleasure is more like bondage to self. Sitting all day and watching Netflix is comfortable but offers little lasting pleasure. The pleasure doesn't last. Take a vacation for example. You have a great time exhausting yourself on vacation looking at museums, beaches, grave sites, etc. When you get home, it is just another memory. True happiness is spiritual happiness knowing you've helped someone overcome depression, sadness, addiction, anxiety, etc., knowing you've made a difference in the world and in someone's life. Yes, happiness is limiting yourself (your ego) to help others. It's also about completion. When you complete a task or project, you feel a sense of happiness, that you accomplished something.

We view happiness as an elusive goal that only the few and fortunate will ever achieve like people who make a million dollars, weigh 110 pounds, look beautiful, own THINGS, and enjoy the gourmet life. The problem is once the need for material possessions is filled the joy is gone. Once the plate is empty, the joy is over. Then, if you're sober and still not happy, you turn to art, music, nature, beautiful objects that adorn our homes and lawns and feel a sense of belonging. But soon that fades because, while you may live within view of the most beautiful one, they will always remain outside of you. Even if you own the Mona Lisa, you will never BE the Mona Lisa because the person who paints the picture experiences a totally different level of joy than the person who buys the picture.

The essence of happiness is the experience of completion; the unrelenting search for what is missing. We are totally dependent on one another, on the physical world, and on our own Higher Power. This dependence: This inner yearning for spiritual completion breeds *character traits* (qualities) within you like humility, gratitude, mutual responsibility, and ultimately JOY. Therefore, spirituality; the unrelenting yearning to complete our own human character is what ultimately brings joy.

The Hebrew word for "happy" (msameach) means being fulfilled and established. A person who is happy with what he enjoys the world more than simply accumulating wealth. A happy person lacks nothing—he is simply happy. A person who bases his essence on his wealth always wants more and compares himself to people who have more than he does. His quality of life is in the work of his own hands. And this is more precious than accumulated more "things."

Case Study: What I've Missed by Always Working

What have I missed because of my preoccupation of not living in the present moment? I mourn not the work I missed but the fun. I missed playing the flute, resting, walking, yoga, getting along better with children. In a sense, I still mourn the disconnection where I've put up barriers to push others away or block their way into my soul. I've missed feeling normal, happy, serene, and powerful. Instead, life is a struggle of the mind to refute irrational bombardments of thought and replace them with aspirational affirmations. Oh, what solace it is being able to cherish positive thoughts and attitudes. There is no time for rest when you're always tired of living; there is time for joy when living has meaning. Addiction and depression take so much from me, I mourn living this kind of life… unappreciative of the blessings I have and cursed by the voices of instant gratification.

Exercises:

What are your goals for yourself and your family? _____
_____

If you want to go back to work, what is the reason? _____
_____

Are you living a balanced life?   Y   N

If not, what can you change? _____

What will bring you true happiness? _____

What else is possible? _____

What could you have done differently? _____

What can I add, subtract, or change in my life to reach my true potential? _____
_____

What does play look like for you? _____

How did you escape the pressures of your life? _____

What makes you curious and excited about life? _____

Who can you teach what you know? _____

How will you feel when you finally get what you want? _____

What are you going to do to get there? _____

How can I allocate my time differently to find more balance in my life?
_____
_____

Reclaiming the Self

Putting Values into Action

Who I want the world to see me as is? _____

Who I really am in the world (my identity, what gives my life meaning)? _____

Where do I find meaning in life? (work, children, partner, religion, heritage, money, power, prestige, music, hobbies, etc.) _____

How can I connect better to others? (the world, the universe, my community, my relation-ships) _____

What parts of yourself have you discarded and disowned? (*I don't/won't* dance, sing, cry, get angry, draw, love, be prejudiced, hate.) _____

I am passionate about _____

A metaphor for my life would be? (Roller coaster, skydiving, stuck in the mud, merry-go-round…)

_____

My inner compass points to the cup being Half Full or Half Empty? _____

Three values I can focus on that will give my life more meaning.

1.
2.
3.

When I am listened to, I feel _____

When I am empowered, having a voice, standing up for myself I feel _____

_____

How do you think the people in your life perceive you? _____

What is your most meaningful relationship? _____

What do YOU need to do to make your relationship more meaningful? _____

_____

What not-private activity gives you the most enjoyment? _____

What is the best decision you ever made? _____

What special thing would you like to accomplish in your lifetime? _____

_____

What is the hardest lesson you've had to learn? _____

What event has given you the most happiness? _____

What event has given you the most anguish? _____

What status symbol would you like to own? Why? _____

What status symbol do you abhor? _____

What question would you like to ask a deceased relative or friend that you did not get a chance to ask (or afraid to ask)? _____

What is the best piece of advice you have ever received? Who gave it to you? Why?

_____

Notes

1 Hope and Freedom is the registered trademark of www.hopeandfreedom.com.
2 A good couple of resources are the books, *The Gift of Rest*, by Joe Lieberman and Sabbath by Wayne Muller.

Section III

Emotions

Chapter 5

Impulsively Exhausting Emotions

The Exodus from Egypt is a central tenant of Judaism. Every year at Passover, millions of Jews around the world sit down and recount the exodus. Why is this message of Egyptian bondage to freedom so central in this religion? It represents the bondage we have to self and to our desires, fueled by our emotions. The purpose today, according to Rabbi Dr. Abraham J. Twerski, in his book, *Teshuva (Repentance) through Recovery*, is to free you from the bondage of the self and learn to serve God instead.

Our ego, or evil inclination, refuses to allow you to serve anyone else but ourselves. We become wrapped up in self and ignore other people's emotions to the point of their feeling a sense of isolation and indifference. No wonder people feel they don't matter.

The question remains, is there true freedom when we serve a Higher Power? There are many laws and ethical teachings that restrict the freedom of the self to do as it pleases, so how is that freedom?

When God gave the Ten Commandments, it says the words were engraved on the tablets. The Hebrew word for engrave is "charus." Charus also means freedom. The point is that the more we are involved in doing what God desires of you, the greater freedom we have over the bondage of self. When we become pure vessels of acceptance, our Higher Power will shine His light upon you, and we will receive His blessings.

Imagine if a blind person were to constantly focus on their disability, they would never have the freedom to develop other skills like a keen sense of hearing, reading braille, and learning to cope with life in ways they never could have imagined like getting married and raising children.

Anxiety

I'll control the situation to avoid being vulnerable and stay in control.

Anxiety today is enslaving you with fear of the future. Work, distractions, and relationships create fertile ground for feeling we have no control over anything in our lives. We are constantly asking "what if this happens," what if we're involved in a catastrophe, what's going to be with my future?" In my practice, I see patients every day who worry about future events they cannot control. This fear of loss of control enslaves them with inaction, procrastination, and a feeling of numbness and isolation. Fertile ground for anxiety, addictive thinking, depression, and acting impulsively.

The truth is we cannot control our future. We can plan and dream all day long, but in the end, nature seems to throw you a curve ball sometimes and we've missed the flight of a life worth living. The antidote is that we do have to put in the effort to get ahead; to plan, to dream, and to implement. As Julia Cameron says in Artist Way, *"You plan, and God will be the judge of the outcome."*

DOI: 10.4324/9781003453185-8

Therefore, <u>giving up control</u>, putting our faith in the hands of our Higher Power, and working toward implementing our plans and dreams is the key to freedom from worry. I do the work and God judges the work. And if my efforts are meant to be, they will bear fruit. If they're not meant to be, understand that where you are in life today is where you're supposed to be. Make the most of every day by putting in effort to make your life worth living. When you can achieve this high level of existence and faith, nothing will get in your way and you'll enjoy the freedom of trusting a Higher Power who is in control of nature and your future.

Exercise:

What are three areas in your life where you could practice surrendering and intentionally release a little more control?

_____   _____   _____

<u>Worrying</u> is a futile attempt at control. What we conceive and believe we can achieve. And if we're constantly believing we are going to fail, or procrastinating, worrying we won't be perfect, we are just setting ourselves up for failure. But, if we can conceive of a life without failure and look at every outcome as a lesson, we will achieve freedom from worry.

Exercise:

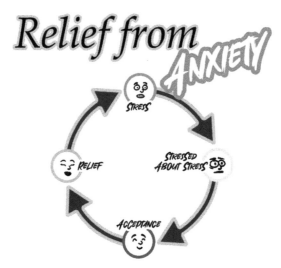

Relief from ANXIETY

STRESS
An anxiety provoking issue that leads to uncomfortable bodily feelings such as worry, fear, heart racing, queasy stomach, sweating, feeling overwhelmed.

STRESSED ABOUT STRESS
An anxiety provoking issue that leads to uncomfortable bodily feelings such as worry, fear, heart racing, queasy stomach, sweating, feeling overwhelmed.

ACCEPTANCE
Accepting stress as a normal emotion instead of a dangerous catastrophe that might happen gives some relief.

RELIEF
Relief occurs when acceptance is coupled with tools that include deep breathing, meditation, mindfulness, yoga. Also, the realization that you cannot control the future so why worry about it. Trust that where you are is where you are supposed to be.

Relief from Anxiety Illustration

Social anxiety is an added component of generalized anxiety disorder. Social anxiety is more about the social aspect but also about an intense fear of being judged. Technology can be both a help and a hindrance to people with social anxiety. Some people use technology as an escape into a fantasy world because reality is just too painful. On the other hand, people can learn to communicate and support each other in groups designed for this purpose. Unfortunately, social media sometimes makes things worse because people with social anxiety are already defensive about judgment and now, they are comparing themselves to everyone on social media who falsely portray their great life of happiness and success.

Exercise:

Consider a social media fast

You will get maximum dopamine rush benefit by initiating a social media fast. Close or pause your social media accounts for a week. At the end of the week, see how you feel. If you're still alive (and you will be), you might realize that you can get by in life without social media and the world will not come to an end. Tell your friends you are fasting for a week from social media, What's App, dating sights, and any apps that take you away from the people you care about and care about you.

Depression and Anger

Depression as it relates to being enslaved to an emotion is really *"anger turned inward."* When we don't express anger outwardly, we hold it in hoping it will simply go away. Usually, it doesn't just go away but festers in our subconscious and turns into resentment toward the person we are angry at. We hold on to these resentments as they pile up, and we end up feeling depressed.

According to Hilary Jacobs Hendel, author of *It's Not Always Depression, "sometimes it's not depression but a reflection of our internal struggle to express our feelings."* Instead, we use all kinds of defense mechanisms to hide our anger and other emotions like shame, guilt, and anxiety that thwart our attempts to fix the problem. Defenses protect you from feeling pain, fear, and hurt. They convince you that it's better to store our feelings into a brain compartment and leave them there, so we don't have to relive these emotions. Defenses can be addiction, vagueness, passivity, low self-esteem, judging, and comparing. Anything we use to convince ourselves not to express our emotions.

There are several **warning signs** that feed depression. When a person feels lonely, they need to seek out people instead of isolating. Sitting around and doing nothing, thinking of your problems, past mistakes, lack of friends, money, keeps you feeling depressed. Stop asking so many "why" questions, like "Why is this happening to me?," "Why can't I get out of this funk?," "Why can't I do anything right?"

Exercise: What Are Your Warning Signs That Feed Depression?

Examples:	Your choices
Isolation	_____
Reliving Your Past, thinking you can change it	_____
Obsessing over problems	_____
Obsessing over past mistakes	_____
Lack of Friends	_____
Lack of Money	_____
Asking *why* instead of taking action	_____

People shame themselves by saying words to themselves like *always, never, must and should* *"I should have done this... I shouldn't have done that, I'm always screwing up, I'll never amount to anything, I must be an...."*

Shame without action keeps you feeling down and angry at yourself. Unless we take opposite action against these shaming thoughts, we will constantly be stuck in shame and depression. The problem is, when we're depressed, we don't want to get out of bed, exercise, meditate, or do anything but sit around and mope. It's a Catch-22 situation. The only way to fix it is to do the opposite of what you feel like doing; exercise, meditate, household chores, hobbies, something to get your mind off the misery and your body up and motivated to action. **Remember Mood Follows Action.**

Here are some common unrealistic thinking errors we sometimes fall into:

1. **If Only.** "Things would be better if only I had more money, more friends, more education, a better job, a better marriage, a different family." Things change when we act, not by sitting around feeling sorry for ourselves.
2. **Wallowing in self-pity** demanding attention and sympathy from others instead of being willing to help ourselves. Self-pity disguises anger, resentment, fear, envy, jealousy, guilt, procrastination, and impatience. Sometimes people are too proud to seek help.
3. Many people carry childlike ideas into adulthood like **the need to control everything and everybody to feel in control** and to fulfill all our needs. Expecting instant gratification without considering consequences can lead to deepening depression as we search desperately for power and attention.
4. **Comparing ourselves to others** and judging ourselves and others, feeds the negative voice that prolongs our depression.
   Consider the following: "Would you let anyone else put you down to the extent that you put yourself down?" Self-hatred and low self-esteem create unnecessary hurdles in our quest to release the bonds of depression. But **the more we use negative talk about ourselves; it becomes a self-fulfilling prophecy.** As the expression goes, *"if you think you can or you think you can't, you're right." Our attitude determines our altitude!*
5. Who is really in control? We always lose when we try to control people, places, and things. We cannot have peace of mind when we're constantly trying to get everyone else to do things our

way. When our inflated ego is directing the play, we set ourselves up for disappointment and become dependent on outside forces for our happiness. Let go of trying to control your future. Accept that what is happening in your world today is what is supposed to be happening and you cannot control what will happen tomorrow. When you live this way, without reliving your past or worrying about your future, you will have serenity, peace of mind, and happiness.

Why We Get Angry

We get angry when our unrealistic demands are not met. When things are not going the way, we think they should. And, until our demands are met, we usually stay stuck in our anger for long periods of time.

In our minds, the demands sound like "shoulds" and "musts." For example, "I must always be perfect," "The world must treat me fairly," "I should be entitled to do whatever I want, despite the consequences to other people."

When events happen that we are not expecting, we become angry or full of rage. These feelings then lead to attacking, defending, or retreating. We may even hurt ourselves by losing sleep, overeating, bodily aches and pains, or addictive behavior.

Unmet desires tend to lead to less intense stress, such as disappointment, sadness, irritation, frustration, etc. Restate your demand as a wish or desire and you will experience less stress, and in turn be able to have a more appropriate response.

Exercise:

Practice restating your demand as a wish.

I wish _____

I wish _____

I wish _____

I wish _____

I wish _____

Another way to think about a situation is to play the tape out of the last time you reacted this way and assess the consequences. A significant part of anger results from our being unwilling to face reality about ourselves, other people, and the world at large. In other words, we continue to be upset about not being perfect, others don't care for you, the world isn't fair, not having enough money and people who continue their bad habits in public.

The answer is acceptance. When we can accept reality, we become less stressed out. Acceptance doesn't mean we're happy about past events that happened to you, or circumstances that are happening today. But we realize that we cannot change other people, situations, or circumstances. It's our attitude toward those circumstances that determines our mental health. When we take the energy consumed in being resentful and adapting it to what we can change and achieve, we remain free of anger.

When we become angry, we wish things were different than they are. To lessen anger it would help to give up our demands, acknowledge our desires, and lower our expectations.

The Serenity Prayer
God, Grant me the serenity to accept the things I cannot change,
The courage to change the things I can,
And the wisdom to know the difference.

Methods for Managing Anger

- You are angry for a reason you create.
- Dispute unrealistic expectations of others.
- Judge a person's behavior, not the person themselves.
- Give people the benefit of the doubt.
- Accept your anger as normal. Pledge to work on reducing intensity and frequency. Accept yourself for being human.
- Practice radical acceptance. Acceptance of reality within body, mind, and soul. This does not mean approval. It means it's not worth carrying around resentments over something that may be meaningless in a few weeks or months.
- Use "I" statements to become more assertive, rather than angry or aggressive.
  Use this formula:

  - When you_____(come home late and don't call).
  - I feel _____ (scared, disrespected, angry).
  - And in the future (I would appreciate it if you would call and let me know you will be late).
  - And if you don't (I will not leave dinner out for you any longer).

- Play the tape out. Say to yourself, last time I got angry I ended up punching a hole in the wall or getting into a physical fight. Is it really worth it, now, to risk having this happen again, or can I stay calm and be assertive rather than aggressive?
- Reward yourself for acting less angrily.
- Write out behavioral contracts with loved ones to eliminate hostility.
- Use humor to defuse situations without being sarcastic and hostile. Lighten up and don't take life so seriously.

How to Deal with an Anger Trigger

Ask yourself the following questions:

- Is this really going to matter tomorrow, next week, or next month?
- Why do I have to have things my way all the time? Do I know anyone who has to put up with uncomfortable situations that they cannot change?
- What is the benefit to me for becoming upset or angry at this person or situation? If there is no benefit, aside from ego gratification, what can I do to let go of it?
- Has your anger response in the past been helpful or harmful to your relationship?
- If you had to do it over again, how would you react now?

- Are you reacting too quickly? Would it be better to remain silent or be more assertive?
- Is the situation really that serious that it's worth jeopardizing your relationship because some petty situation is not going YOUR WAY?
- What is the advantage for holding on to my anger? What are the advantages of letting go? Do a pros and cons analysis to review both sides?
- What do you need now, to let go of your displeasure, even if letting go is temporary?

Excerpted from The Therapist's Assistant audiotape. Philadelphia: Media Psychology Associates, 1996.

Healthy Anger

- Observing and experiencing anger without being overwhelmed by it.
- Recognizing anger as a signal to explore feelings, thoughts, and bodily reactions.
- Recognizing anger as a signal to turn inward and identify core desires, needs, and values.
- Developing a sense of compassion for ourselves and others.
- Consider forgiveness of ourselves and others.
- Learning how to communicate effectively and assertively so we don't succumb to holding on to resentments.

  - Say to yourself: Nothing can steal my joy
  - What people think of me is none of my business
  - Other people are responsible for their own actions
  - I am responsible for my reaction
  - How can I grow stronger and wiser?

- Use a spiritual practice like mindfulness or meditation, yoga, etc. to express emotions through body movement and mind control.
- Take productive action toward completing a project or task that will give you a sense of accomplishment and purpose in life. Concentrate on these things rather than insignificant events and people who rob you of your vitality.

(Excerpted with permission from Healthy Anger: A Mind and Body Approach, Bernard Golden, Ph.D. Counselor Magazine, August 2017).

Resentments

In Ecclesiastes, Chapter 11:9 it says, *"Rejoice young man in your youth and let your heart cheer you in the days of your youth, and walk in the ways of your heart, and in the sight of your eyes, but know that for all these things God will bring you to judgment."*

Resentments are the addict's number one offender. Holding on to resentments is like swallowing poison, then waiting for the other person to die.

Here's a letter from a client who holds on to resentment and then rationalizes his actions to act out:

Part of me says, *"I can't stand it anymore, I have to act out"* or *"If I only can do it one more time, that will save me." "I just want to look one more time, go to that place one more time."* I know that is my addiction talking. How do I overcome this? I ask myself, *"Do I really want to go back to secretly sneaking around, lying to my family, covering myself up so no one will see me? Do I really want to go through this pain of withdrawal all over again?"* NOOOOOO!!!!!!

Once a person lets their guard down, it's easy to rationalize and say, "I can do this on my own." And then they fall.

King Solomon gives you the answer in Ecclesiastes (11:10). *"Therefore, remove anger (resentment, fear) from your heart, and put away evil from your flesh, for childhood and youth are vanity."* This is the answer. *"Remove resentment, fear and anger from your heart."* For many people, resentment is the #1 cause of falling. We're not talking about emotional, physical, or sexual abuse here. Such people need professional help. We're talking about everyday annoyances that we blow out of proportion, and they affect you negatively by shutting you down.

Exercise: Resentment Atom

List Resentments then fill in the resentment atom to go deeper

Shame vs. Guilt

We are wounded in private and healed in public

Many people confuse shame and guilt as being the same emotion. They are very different. Guilt is doing something against our values or morals; or in religious terms, a sin. Shame is "I am a bad person because of what I did, or just a bad person because that's what I was told."

Guilt can be corrected by being in the same situation again and not acting on it. We show remorse for our actions and resolve not to do it again. This is the way of repentance from guilt.

Shame, on the other hand, is a bit tricky. When we use words against ourselves or others, like *must, should, always,* and *never*, we are shaming, and it stings like an arrow through our entire being and remains there until we can reframe the shame. There is a concept of healthy shame. It's what stops you from doing things we know are against our values and moral compass. Healthy shame builds humility, reduces arrogance, and makes you more socially conscious human beings. Unhealthy shame causes you to feel humiliated and dominated by feelings of inadequacy. When we don't know how to deal with our shame it becomes another justification for behaving against our core values. It changes our reality into thinking we are deficient in some way, when actually we have many positive traits to define ourselves.

Everyone experiences shame during their lifetime. Like any emotion, it comes and goes but when it is severe it can be very painful. We all have our own person triggers that create shame and what we do with that feeling determines its intensity. Toxic shame hangs around for awhile and causes you to have a low self-image, perfectionism, and codependency. It creates feelings of inadequacy and anxiety and can spiral down into depression and feelings of hopelessness and helplessness. If toxic shame is not healed, it can also lead to aggression, eating disorders, PTSD, and addiction.

There is a relationship between shame, anger, and fear. Imagine an iceberg. Peeking up through the water is the tip of the iceberg, which represents shame. We hold onto shame because it's embarrassing to be vulnerable enough to admit we have a flaw. Under the surface of the water, spread out wide and clear are the foundations of the iceberg, anger, and fear. Shame covers up the anger and fear we feel that we don't want to express. The problem is if you don't reveal your true self by talking about shame, others will reinvent you and you may not like what they come up with!

Exercise:

Ways I feel badly about what I did: _____

_____

Ways I feel badly about who I am _____

_____

Shame, anger and fear: Your identity

Adversity and Fear

Sidney Howard said, *"You become what you fear. Half of knowing what I want is knowing what I must give up to get it."* When a tree's root system is weak, the tree is at risk of toppling over. When it is strong, the tree branches and leaves can withstand strong winds and survive. Adversity strikes all of you, but when we possess a strongly rooted system of acting properly, doing good deeds, it strengthens you to be able to withstand adversity.

The Maharal of Prague, a Jewish mystic and philosopher in the 16th century writes, *"The burden of great theoretical knowledge can render a person unable to deal with adversity, if his root system is shallow."* Therefore, when life becomes difficult, using only an intellectual approach makes it easy to rationalize inappropriate behavior to escape adversity. But when we are doing the right thing by practicing good deeds, we are less likely to rationalize inappropriate behavior because we've **practiced good deeds** and they become a part of our spiritual essence to continue to do what is right.

Exercise:

Growing up what did you dream of becoming? _____

Growing up what did you fear you might become? _____

Like your parent? An addict? A failure? _____

What does doing the right thing mean to you? _____

How do you define integrity, both generally and personally? _____

Is it possible to learn how to proceed WITH fear instead of becoming paralyzed by fear?
_____

Write about an experience you've had where you were paralyzed by fear and did it anyway.
_____
_____
_____

Who Is Causing Your Suffering?

Are you causing your own suffering? Pain plus non-acceptance equals suffering. When you are constantly fighting reality saying, "it's hopeless," "this shouldn't have happened," or "I'm never going to amount to anything," you are only creating more suffering for yourself. When you don't accept reality, when you sit around and do nothing, you simply create more suffering. When you simply ignore life and make no effort to accomplish anything, you're only hurting yourself. People who live with adversity and fear turn to drugs, alcohol, self-harm, eating binges, sex, and gambling to escape the pain of the shameful messages they keep telling themselves.

Have you ever noticed that some people who experience adversity bounce back right away, and others keep the resentment and anger bottled up for years? Some people have a hard time dealing with negative emotions and they can't "just get over it." The people who bounce back face reality and are willing to participate fully in the world.

According to Marsha Linehan, Ph.D., founder of Dialectical Behavior Therapy, "When you want to let go of your suffering, you have to radically accept the following:

1. Life's reality is what it is.
2. There is a cause to everything that happens.
3. We can create a life worth living and still have pain.

To solve a problem in your life you have four choices:

1. Change it
2. Fix it
3. Accept it the way it is
4. Stay miserable

When you have a negative emotion and don't accept it, it festers within you, and you become a negative and ambivalent person. In other words, when you are unwilling to sit with and accept a feeling, you tend to escape into behaviors like drugs, alcohol, sex, gambling, shopping, etc. to avoid the feeling. This unwillingness to sit with the feelings leads to cloudy thinking and behaviors, which cause you to feel guilt and shame. It becomes a vicious cycle because the only way we know to get rid of stress, guilt, and shame is to numb out the feeling instead of accepting it and letting it pass. But when we numb out negative feelings, we also close ourselves off to happiness and joy.

On the other hand, when we accept the negative emotion and can simply sit with it until it dissipates, we practice opening ourselves up to accepting the discomfort. It's just a feeling. It's not dangerous; it's just annoying. We are willing to face the challenge and simply notice ourselves slowing down to observe our feelings and thoughts and bring awareness to our values, morals, and beliefs. Our emotions rise like waves in the ocean. They peak and then fall. It's our willingness to sit with the emotion until it weakens, which promotes acceptance and self-care.

Maimonides claims the cure for fear is trust in a Higher Power. He states: *"For whatever a man thinks is hurting him, and it brings sadness and mourning, it can only be for two reasons: Either he meditates upon the past; losing money, a family death, or he meditates on what is going to happen in the future and imagines he will suffer a loss. It is known through intellectual observation that ruminating over the past will be of no avail in any way and these are the actions of people who lack intellect."*

Psalms (37:3) states, *"trust in God and do good; dwell in the land and cultivate faith...his heart should tryout securely in God, and he should not fear the future and what it may bring."* The opposite of fear is having the courage to tryout in God because we cannot control the future. Some people are born with a predisposition to fear. Everyone experiences fear, frustration, insecurity, resentment, and discontent. It's having the courage to push through the fear and accept the fact we have no control over the future, so why worry?

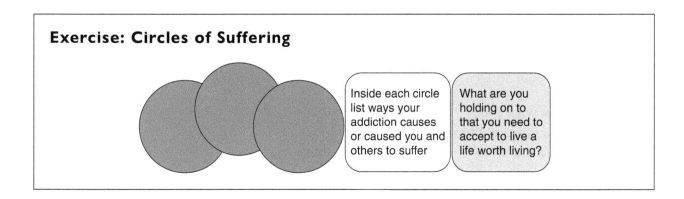

Envy, Desire, and Honor

Ethics of the Fathers 4:28 says, *"Envy, Desire, and Honor remove a person from this world."* What do we gain and lose when we remain envious of others? Our purpose in the world is to harness our energy in increasing peace and well-being in the world. Envy, desire, and honor make self-interest our sole purpose causing you to clash with the rest of the world; our only value being our own self-interest. Jealousy brings one to envy. According to the Maharal of Prague, "jealousy is associated with the spiritual, while desire or lust is associated with the body. The evil inclination originates from this physical craving for lust." But, according to the Path of the Just, Chapter 11, *envy is nothing but ignorance and foolishness, since the envious one does not gain anything for himself, nor does he harm the one he envies.* He only harms himself as it says in Job 5, *"And envy slays the gullible."*

It's the old story of the clash between intellect and desire, emotions vs. logic. Intellect begs you to consider the consequences of our desirous actions but when we are caught in the web of desire, we throw consequences out the window. We want instant gratification, right now and don't care what happens next. But it becomes a vicious cycle because once we act on our desires, we feel guilt and shame and the only way we know to rid ourselves of guilt and shame is to fulfill our desires again. The trick is to step back and consider what good we will experience when we don't give in to desire or envy. "The goodwill" can be tranquility, emotional sobriety and serenity, and relief from the darkness, which causes you sadness, hurt, and a bruised self-image. "Evil" is recurring worry, sorrow, and constant grieving of not being able to control ourselves, without the help of others. The need for honor stops you from seeking help.

Relational Affect

Sylvan Tomkins' affect theory states that "affect is the innate, biological response to the increasing, decreasing, or persistent intensity of neural firing. This results in a particular feeling, facial and body display, and skin changes. Affects feel rewarding, punishing, or neutral in their own ways. Affect makes things urgent.

> Awareness of an affect is a feeling. ***"A feeling plus memory of prior similar feelings is an emotion."***

A child who comes from a family where they are dismissed, rejected, and pyouhed away emotionally, does not learn how to relate emotionally and usually shuts down. When boys begin to show emotions, studies show parents will give them something to distract them; a toy, watch TV, go outside, and they often don't develop the skills to express emotions. *They become "normatively alexithymia lacking the ability to identify the feeling state, identify it and for this reason struggle with how to use the feeling. The feelings are experienced in the body and for this reason they turn to bodily means to address it, leaving them susceptible to substance and behavioral addictions (Crocker, 2015).*

Dr. Michael Crocker, a psychotherapist in New York, explains that you have biographical scripts of emotions; sadness, anger, fear, stress, disgust, and shame. When a person feels these emotions, they have an urge to escape the negative emotion script, try to get out of the negativity and this results in acting out with food, liquor, drugs, sex, gambling, shopping, video games, etc.

When you cannot identify the emotional script, you will eventually act out, becoming enslaved to your form of medicating yourself. Additionally, as Tomkins has noted,

> we often become familiar to our Affect Script, and that change becomes uncomfortable, like a stranger we do not tryout. So, when we gain **hope, love and playfulness,** we can be at risk of slipping and relapse as our distress, fear, anger and/or shame scripts harken you back to where we were most comfortable. Erdman and Crocker (2019) called these **"Idioms of Attachment"** - manners in which attachment, as maladaptive as the attachment strategy may be, is familiar, and feels like we are home. Change comes slowly through "corrective emotional experiences" with good therapists, sponsors and loving peers. One step at a time. **John Bowlby stated clearly: That which we do not get we become allergic to.** The Sexuality, Attachment and Trauma Project Model of treatment is much like treating allergies - we expose those who have been neglected and or abused to the compassion they have become allergic to, in order to help them tolerate the allergen, even when the allergen is love, care, hope and compassion.

Exercise:

Take an inventory as to your relationship with play instead of work.

When did you feel the best? _____

Watch the movie "*Inside Out*"

Create a "playlist" of hobbies, things you can create and complete, games, and healthy distractions.

_____   _____   _____
_____   _____   _____
_____   _____   _____
_____   _____   _____

   List positive elements of what you're hopeful for, what and who you love and who you can engage in more play with:

_____
_____
_____

   Causes of Slipping and Relapse:

Distress _____

Fear _____

Anger _____

Shame _____

Areas of abuse or neglect _____

Roots of Emotional Distress

An addiction is an obsession or compulsion that a person cannot control, although they think they can and it begins to affect them and others physically, emotionally, and spiritually.

Most addictions—work, gambling, drinking, or food—are a spiritual malady of wanting to fill a void in a person's soul. They are triggered to act out when they feel angry, resentful, bored, lonely, tired, or fearful. Addictions have their roots in emotional distance from caregivers in early childhood, heredity, abuse, and trauma. Your addiction talks you into acting out when your body and mind tell you you're innocent. This devil and angel conversation constantly goes on in our minds. One inclination is to do what's right, according to your belief system. The evil inclination rationalizes and justifies our compulsions, telling you one more time won't hurt anything or anyone, you deserve it, or you're entitled because you work so hard.

Here is an actual case of a young person struggling with an addiction to pornography.

When I was struggling with porn, I felt my evil inclination was literally pulling and pounding my head in any direction that he wished. It was as if I had no free choice. The reason I felt like this is because…this IS what was happening. He was in control. Wherever I would walk, I tried and failed. Then, I decided to make very, very small goals. I would accept upon myself, that the walk from down the street to my home, I absolutely no matter what, would not look anywhere except at the ground. It was difficult, but this was a goal that I could handle. After a few times of doing this, I was able to increase the goal. During the same period when I was driving, which is much more difficult as we are looking almost everywhere in order to drive safely, I could see with my peripheral vision, that there were "interesting" things walking on the sidewalk. I literally had to scream and shout with pain in order to break the pull of the desire to look. This too worked, and immediately afterwards things became much easier.

The disease of addiction will always haunt the addict. They will always be tempted, and it just gets easier to cope when you have the tools to avoid the triggers, which cause you to act out. You live in serenity when you know what to do when you're triggered. But if you constantly live in fear of acting out, clinging on to lustful thoughts, you will eventually fall.

The bottom line is, "what we resist – persists." If we hide in a cave so we will never look at another human being again to avoid lust, you will live in pain. But when you accept the fact that you can look for three seconds and turn away, you release the power of constantly saying, don't look, don't look, don't look, don't look, and it relieves the pain.

> *We don't put our jewelry and our garbage in the same place in our house, why do we put them together in our minds?*

The duty of your subconscious mind is to protect you by answering questions. We're asking ourselves questions all day and our subconscious answers them. Initially, addicts don't know "why" they act out. They've been numb to their feelings for so long, they can't describe how they really feel. So when I ask them, "what triggers you to act out," they have a difficult time answering.

Instead of guessing, it's more helpful to access answers from your subconscious. Simply ask yourself, "What is causing me now to be restless, irritable and discontent?" Ponder it for a while and let it go, the answer will come. If it's resentment, pray for the person to have what you want for yourself. If it's fear, ask God to show you how to tryout HIM more instead of trying to control the future.

As addicts, we tend to overthink everything and sometimes this causes you more anxiety. Acceptance is the key. Feel the feeling, accept it as <u>just</u> a feeling, don't push it away or you give it MORE power. Accept it, take a walk, and think it over. You don't have to do anything when you have a feeling or thought. Accept it as simply a feeling, let it go and think about something else.

You can also look at addiction as an allergy. If you have an allergy you stay away from the cause of the allergy. If your partner had a physical disease, would he talk to the doctor or just wait till he gets really sick and it's too late? Addiction is a progressive disease. He may be looking at porn now but soon that will not be enough and things he may swear he will never do; he will do anyway. That is the nature of addiction.

Keep in mind that when an addict slips back into acting out, they can access the times of sobriety they've experienced, which were clean living and sobriety. Addicts experience the sweetness of this period and no one can take that away from them. So, when you slip, don't assume you've fallen down to the lowest level of the pits. Use it as a learning experience (it's part of the process) and move on. When an addict slips, don't assume they've fallen to the lowest level of the pits. Instead, use it as a learning experience, get up, and move on.

Spirituality, Sin, and Addiction

I wrote a letter to a client confused about spirituality, sin, and addiction:

Everyone who overcomes a sin is a righteous person who repents, and Ecclesiastes says, *there is no man who has not sinned.*

God knew this and that is why HE created repentance. HE knew people would sin.

Spirituality has different meanings to different people. Some people equate it with religion while others simply ignore it, spending their lives searching for meaning. Spirituality is the foundation, the answer, to moving from self-slavery to a life of freedom. The spirit is the part of you that distinguishes you as humans from other forms of life. When we exercise these unique capacities, we are said to being spiritual.

Indulgence in excess is a unique human experience. Animals know when to stop eating and drinking. All they have are their physical urges and desires. Human beings also crave spiritual fulfillment. When this spiritual fulfillment goes haywire, humans become restless. Spiritual craving is harder to identify. People have a hole in their soul that they try to fill up with all sorts of unhealthy habits, when filling your soul with spirituality is the answer.

Here is another letter I wrote to a client…

There is an old saying that "*curiosity killed the cat.*" An addiction is a disease not an intentional sin, but that does not give a person permission to continue doing it because it will ruin their soul. For example, there are plenty of legitimate massage places by licensed therapists given by men that can help a person reduce stress. Your addictive thinking is telling you, "I have to go to a female masseuse."

You have an intimacy disorder, a broken attachment, which keeps you from having a long-lasting relationship. As long as you keep acting out in your addiction, you will have no secure connection to spirituality or women. When you honestly can say you want this connection then you are ready to decide. Either continue to act out and eventually get caught or get into a program where you can get some help and figure out what is causing you to want to jeopardize your life and relationship. Here are some ideas:

Acting out means you are "medicating" anger, resentment, fear, loneliness, boredom, or stress. It's a vicious cycle. When you feel stress, you act out to feel better. Then you feel shame and guilt and act out over and over again to cover up the shame and guilt.

Make the decision right now to turn your will and life over to the care of God as you understand Him. Realize that you are not in control of your future, but there is a power greater than you that is in control of the future. And when you can stop worrying about the future and stop living in the past, you will find serenity and peace of mind and won't need substances or dangerous behaviors to tune out with, thinking you're solving your problems.

Repentance from sin is not that we did something wrong and now we're showing we won't do it again. It's more that doing something against our values brings you down spiritually and repentance is a way to boost you back up.

Exercise: The Feelings Inventory

Feelings just are… they require no action

I needed my parent's love when I _____

When I am emotionally supported I can _____

When I feel other people's, love is based on my performance, I feel _____

In my family, success means _____

The benefit I receive from worrying about my future is _____

If I change that means I will have to _____

If I don't _____, then _____

If I don't _____ then my partner will say _____

When my procrastinating voice says, "It'll be OK, you're fine, don't worry about anything, that voice sounds like my _____.

I wish I weren't so _____

I wish I were more _____

This makes me feel _____

What I can do about it is _____

What I needed from you mom, was _____, what I got was _____

What I needed from you dad, was _____, what I got was _____

More Questions:

What lessons have you learned from your life history? _____

What is the purpose of your existence? _____

Why are you here on earth? _____

Why has a Higher Power seen fit to keep you alive in spite of your shortcomings?

_____

What are the areas you feel you can better yourself? How will you implement these changes? When will you begin?

_____

_____

_____

What would happen if you delayed instant gratification and considered the long-term consequences of your actions? _____

_____

_____

Chapter 6

Driving Determined Decisions

Belief and Decisiveness Inspire Us to Improve Our
Character

A Higher, more powerful force maintains the natural order, so why worry?

Jeanne Guyon says, "*It is not your diligence; it is not your examination of yourself that will en-*
lighten you concerning sin. Instead, it is God who does all the revealing. If you try to be the one
who does the examining, there is a very good chance that you will deceive yourself."

In Ethics of the Fathers 2:13 it says, "*What is the straight path for a man to follow? Rabbi*
Eliezer says, having a good eye." Vision is associated with being able to understand concepts. As it says in Ecclesiastes 1:16, "my heart saw much wisdom and knowledge." In other
words, our hearts are associated with understanding the consequences of our actions (Basser,
2006).

People confuse what they have with who they are and when they lose possessions, nothing
much is left for them to hold on to. Therefore, having a good eye is essential to seeing the good in
ourselves and in other people. Seeing them as human beings instead of how big a house and car
they possess. Things can be lost, but our essence of character will always be with you.

In Ethics of the Fathers 1:15 it says, "*If I am not for myself, who will be for me?*" In other
words, I have to be committed to myself in order to control my feelings of self-importance.

We are constantly told to improve our character and to remove our character defects, but little
is mentioned about what to replace the defects with. Hence, the rest of this chapter will explain
these concepts and show the dichotomy of opposing traits.

Spirituality—Replacing Character Defects

Edward M. Berckman said, "*We are meant to be addicted to God, but we develop secondary ad-*
dictions that temporarily appear to fix our problem."

Spirituality is neither a "thing" nor an object that can be identified as something we possess. It is a process, a growth experience. Ironically, when we think we've achieved spirituality, we have probably lost it because it is a journey, not a destination. We have it as long as
we are striving for it.

Step Six of the Twelve Steps of Alcoholics Anonymous states, "*Were entirely ready to have*
God remove all these defects of character." Step Seven states, "*Humbly asked Him to remove our*
shortcomings."

DOI: 10.4324/9781003453185-9

Recovery is a process of working to improve our character traits and exploring the causes of what has been pulling you toward a bondage to anger, resentment, fear, abandonment, and loneliness.

> *"There is no more effective protection against the danger or deifying the creature than a proper self-appraisal, than being completely permeated with the consciousness of your own task in life."*

According to the authors of *Drop the Rock: Removing Character Defects* (Hazelden, 2005, Center City, MN, 57) humbly asking God to remove our shortcomings begins with humility. Humility is a middle point between grandiosity and shame. You have to know you are worthwhile, but you don't have to go shouting it from the rooftops. It is not being meek, but being grateful for the strengths, skills, and successes you do have.

Dr. Abraham Twerski writes about spirituality in his book, *Self-Improvement? I'm Jewish: Overcoming Self-Defeating Behavior*:

When a person's life is geared toward reaching a spiritual goal, a person can be spiritual 24 hours a day; but a person cannot achieve spirituality alone. Dr. Twerski defines spirituality as a *"striving for something more than satisfaction of our biological urges, being considerate of others and not encroaching on their rights."* Prayer is necessary in asking God to remove our character defects. Our prayers will only be accepted when we embrace an attitude of humility. Vanity and arrogance are abominable traits and a person must humble himself to achieve spiritual assistance. Greed, avarice, lying, and cheating cannot coexist in a spiritual being. When we have no belief system or spirituality, we are not acting out of humility but out of our own capricious impulses.

As Rabbi Samson Rafael Hirsch says in Horeb, Section 1 page 10, *"Both non-belief and sexual promiscuity lead to idolatry. For as soon as enjoyment becomes the object of your life, you no longer regard yourself as belonging to the world but* the world as belonging to you, *and you know no law but your own capricious impulses. From that moment, you will no longer understand what is meant by unselfishness, you will see in every creature a being which only obeys itself and works only for itself."*

Exercise:

What is the difference between religion and spirituality?

What are the most harmful character traits that you notice in other people? (Arrogance, greed, avarice, lying, cheating, promiscuity, vanity, selfishness, envy, shame, hatred, cruelty, worry, anger, laziness, flattery, slander) Why are they so harmful?

If you had to name one character trait that has been a challenge for most of your life, what would that character trait be?

What are you doing spiritually to perfect that trait in your life?

What acts of kindness toward you do you most appreciate?

What is the one missed opportunity you most regret?

How will you know when you've become a more spiritual person?

Who could serve as a spiritual mentor for you?

Faith

The suicide rate in America has been climbing steadily for years, and politicians and medical experts have been searching for novel ways to prevent it. A 2016 study by JAMA Psychiatry found that women who attended some type of religious service at least once a week were five times less likely to commit suicide. A 2019 Pew Research study found that regular participation in a religious community is clearly linked to greater happiness.

We all have a spark of the divine within us, and when we get in touch with that, we feel more secure and spiritual. Houses of worship bring people together to experience spiritual enlightenment.

The drought for meaning in our lives leaves people tied down to unhealthy devices and behaviors that cause more harm than good. They hunger for spiritual meaning in their lives. For thousands of years before the sexual and secular revolutions, people turned to houses of worship to find solace, peace of mind, and meaning in life through faith.

Here is a letter I wrote to a friend who was struggling with spirituality, shame, and faith.

The point is your low self-esteem. You are medicating yourself, so you'll feel better instead of boosting yourself up with spirituality, prayer and forgiveness.

If you say this is normal, and your friends are condoning (and probably doing it themselves) why can't you look people in the eye? There is no one who does not make errors in judgment. Everyone has their own tests. This is yours. Other people have their own challenges. It is no reason to give up. The problem will never go away but it gets a lot easier.

If you really want to get better, you must stop doing it. Get a filter for your phone and computer. Once you stop, God will help you. While you're still doing it, God won't fill you up spiritually because your soul is too full of images.

Instead of asking God for help, thank Him for what you do have, a child, a wife, food, clothing, a job.

You can still put filters on your computer if you're working. And if you need it for school you can use the library in a public place. And if you work for a large company, they have ways of blocking it also. It's all your addiction telling you you're doomed, and you might as well just act out anyway, because it's all hopeless. It's not hopeless. Do the things you're supposed to do to avoid lust and you'll make it.

Don't ever give up. This is not your fault – you're the victim here, but I'm telling you, you can get help. Please don't let religiosity get in the way. The SA groups are to help you stop acting out your addiction. And that will save your life, literally. You must stop to be able to begin thinking clearly enough to begin healing. It's the first step.

Don't copy the behavior and customs of this world,
but let God transform you into a new person
by changing the way, you think. (Romans 12:2 NLT)

Exercise:

What gives your life meaning? _____

List three things in your life you are most grateful for? _____

Of what achievements are you most proud? _____

What special thing would you like to accomplish in your lifetime? _____

What part does faith play in your life? _____

Do you occupy your time reliving your past, worrying about the future or living in the present, just for today? _____

How would you define your life's purpose? _____

Love vs. Indifference

Robert Fulghum says, *"We're all a little weird. And life is a little weird. And when we find someone whose weirdness is compatible with ours, we join up with them and fall into mutually satisfying weirdness—and call it love—true love."*

Hate is not the opposite of love. Indifference is the opposite of love.

The term "true love" implies that there is another kind of love that is not <u>true</u> love. According to Alexandra Katehakis and Tom Bliss in their book, *Mirror of Intimacy*, *"It's a fact of human nature that, due to their own past trauma and hurt, people aren't always as they present themselves."* A good relationship is one where there is mutual respect and kindness. When we define love as respect and kindness, love is critical. But sometimes what we think is love is really neediness and we begin to treat the people we love without respect or kindness. A good relationship is about tryout, acceptance, communication, and a genuine liking of the other person with a willingness to compromise. Good relationships are not about constant closeness and smothering of affection.

Love does not mean the same thing to everyone. Some people feel loved when you help them around the house, others like touch or affirmations to make them feel like a priority. Some people feel loved when you spend quality time with them, while others might prefer gifts.

People experience love in different ways. People who grow up with secure attachment to caregivers, experience love as passion, intimacy, and intensity. They want to be emotionally and physically close and show their love with kindness and consideration.

People who have an anxious attachment style experience love as out of control and lose their identity by overwhelming themselves with worry. They become impulsive and needy, fall in love quickly and love begins to consume them. These people make rash decisions and are easily taken advantage of.

People with a dismissing attachment view love as a game of conquest of other people's emotions. They gain control by manipulation and their lovers are caught up in the web of gaslighting, outwitting their partners, and exploiting their weaknesses. Lying and cheating are common and are just part of the game.

The opposite of love is indifference. A person just really doesn't care what the other person thinks or feels. They are so wrapped up in themselves, taking instead of giving, that you are no longer their priority. Their priorities are work and distractions, while family and friends get pushed to the side and ignored.

Another form of indifference is reacting to the world out of rote. I do the same thing over and over again for years and it becomes so second nature that I can do it in my sleep. The problem is that it's fake. And when you're faking life, trying to impress people with your outward righteousness, you're merely putting on a mask. You're presenting yourself one way to the outside world, knowing inside you really don't care if you put in a concentrated effort to focus on what you're doing. It's all a show to distract from your lack of enthusiasm for life with a fake façade of trying to fit in with what everyone else is doing. And while you're thinking you're faking everyone out with your outward arrogance, the façade begins to crumble under the pressure of finally facing the truth of what drives you and who you really are.

Exercise:

How do you define love? _____

What areas of your life are you indifferent about? _____

What are some things you do out of rote (habit without thinking)? _____

What are you anxious about in your relationship? _____

What feelings do you avoid out of fear of rejection or conflict? _____

What part of you believes your relationship is like a game to be played with other's emotions?

_____

Generosity vs. Deprivation

Deprivation corrodes the soul with the toxicity of shame. Shame erodes hope and joy. Deprivation uses obsession to put order in the world. People accept less than they deserve all the time. Deprivation becomes an existential position in life. Being deprived makes addiction look good and deserving. When illness deprives us of certain functionality, we are faced with the reality that we can no longer enjoy certain pleasures we once cherished. But we can learn something from deprivation and that is to make the most of what we do have and choose to make the most of our abilities, strengths, and attitude. A person can be deprived of a job and, at the same time, have a wife who supports him in his efforts to pursue his dreams. A person can be deprived of being mentally healthy, yet function and help others, which ultimately brings fulfillment.

When we monetize our experiences, we deprive ourselves of the joy of giving. Why is it not enough to feel good about ourselves and our abilities? When we help someone and expect nothing in return, we are practicing generosity, even though we think we are depriving ourselves of money. Deprivation is an unconscious fear of success because even if we are more successful it will never be enough.

Diligence vs. Laziness

Having a focus on one thought leads to success. So many people allow hundreds of thoughts to swirl around in their minds, subjugating them to stress and laziness. When we don't have focus, we have a natural human tendency to fall or simply do nothing. As the Talmud states: *"In a place that a person is determined to go, God helps him get there."* Focus helps you figure out right from wrong instead of allowing your evil inclination (negative voice) to turn against you.

For example, a client presents with a variety of "problems." Physical illness, stress, depression, communication issues with their spouse and all these thoughts are swirling around in their minds, crippling them from taking any action. As I attempt to help the person with everything I suggest, the client says they can't do it. That's a form of laziness. They are not willing to consider a different position. They are stuck in the comfort of doing nothing and hoping someone comes along and bails them out of life.

Rationalization, denial, and entitlement convince you we can go ahead and act against our better judgment. It is human nature to be lazy. A lazy person will reinforce their position to the extent of complete irrationality and distort reality to convince himself he can put it off until tomorrow. We convince ourselves we must live comfortably, by rationalizing our inaction to fulfill our prophecy.

Proverbs 26 states, *"A lazy person is wise in his own eyes, more than seven smart advisors who give excellent advice."* He feels he is smarter than them. His laziness does not allow him to even consider what people tell him otherwise. He is the only one who has the wisdom to know what is right.

Sobriety and Serenity—What's the Difference?

Serenity is the destination on the Journey to Hope and Freedom, a sense of emotional integrity and resilience. Sobriety is only the first step on the journey. Faith, letting go of resentments, improving our character, making amends, regularly taking personal inventory, and helping others, lead you to the freedom of serenity. Therefore, while a person may be sober and not acting out with alcohol, drugs, sex, gambling, technology, food, or shopping, until they can regulate their emotions when life throws them a curveball, they are like dry drunks. The term "dry drunk" refers to a person who is no longer drinking but is still angry, resentful, anxious, and miserable, as if he were still acting out. That state of mind is not serenity.

I wrote to a porn-addicted client about the differences in sobriety and serenity:

It's easy to tell you what to do, but until you experience sobriety for a while you will never get to feel the joy of serenity. I've told many people to put filters on their computer. They cry to me that they must stop looking and ask me "what can I do?" But when I recommend putting a filter on their computer their answer is "No, I'm not ready for that."

There are chemical imbalances in the brain caused by watching inappropriate videos on the internet. If you don't believe it, explain to me why it is so hard to stop. And why are there withdrawal symptoms where you shake and sweat? Psychologically, when you know you don't have access, you eventually forget about it. I'm not saying you will never think about it, but the filter is an essential tool to help you heal and get better at the beginning of the process.

Serenity is a quest for spirituality. The lack of serenity is really a "lack of spirituality." Addicts are constantly looking outside themselves for validation, acceptance, and companionship… for intimacy. But true intimacy is sharing everything, being vulnerable and not hiding your feelings from those you love. How long do you want to continue living a lie, to keep covering up everything you do so your wife won't find out? Eventually she will and then it will be too late.

Continue to mourn the pain you've been through. Put it in the past. There is nothing you can do about it anymore. The future is up to a Higher Power. Just concentrate on today, this minute and appreciate the little things. That's the key to serenity.

A lot of times as we approach a goal or a victory in life, we tend to sabotage ourselves (fear of success) because we've always been told we were not good enough. How can I achieve anything if I'm not good enough? That's just your evil inclination talking. Talk back to it in your mind and tell yourself why you <u>are</u> good enough. You're a good father, hyouband, friend, you help other people, and you're an asset in your community. Your parents didn't know the real you anyway, in the past. Now the real you is coming out and you can begin to appreciate the little things you do have.

Give yourself a break and pamper yourself a little. To hell with the rest of the world. It's time to take that huge globe called the world off your shoulder, put it down and let someone else worry about everything and everyone else. You deserve it.

Choosing the Middle Path

Maimonides, a Medieval Rabbi, Doctor, and Philosopher, explains how a person can bring about change in his character (which he describes as a "cure"). He says:

And how may their cure be? He who is of a hot temperament should be taught to humble himself. If he is smitten or cursed, he must not feel the insult at all and follow this path until anger is completely rooted out from his heart. And he who is arrogant should accustom himself to a life of extreme self-abasement…. And this line he should follow in all his tendencies, if he has distanced himself to the extreme of one, he should remove himself to the extreme end of the other and follow it up a long time until he may return to the good way, which is the middle path in each and every tendency.

Choosing the middle path and avoiding extremes helps you earn the esteem of others. People who can compromise and accept people with different opinions live a much happier, more fulfilled life. Stingy people may think highly of their ability to accumulate wealth, but do not earn the respect of other people. On the other hand, a generous person may be popular, but he may impoverish himself by always trying to be in control politically.

Exercise:

How do you define spirituality for yourself?_____

What does your faith teach you about forgiveness? _____

How indifferent are you in your romantic relationship? _____

How indifferent are you in your family relationship? _____

Work relationships? _____

What does the middle path look like for you? _____

Which character traits do you need to improve? _____

How will you improve them? _____

What gets in the way of you being more generous with your time? _____

With your money? _____

With your family? _____

Section IV

People

Chapter 7

The Indifference of Annoying People

Turcois Ominek once said, "*Your time is way too valuable to be wasting it on people that can't accept who you are.*" Genesis 1:26 states, "*Let you make mankind in our image, in our likeness, and let them have dominion over the fish of the sea, and over the birds of the air and over the cattle and over all the earth.*" The Maharal of Prague explains that the image of God is a spark that flows from Him and infuses itself into each person. This radiance is the essence of all existence. Full existence is associated with autonomy. A person who is controlled by another person does not have a complete personal existence because he lives partly within another's control.

When people annoy you, we give them permission to control our thoughts and feelings. We lose our autonomy to make our own decisions. We have to get to the point of feeling secure with ourselves; to not allow others' actions to spoil our spiritual existence.

Social Media's Effect on Youth

My self-worth is dependent on what others think about me

Depression and anxiety among youth are rising. A nationwide study on pediatrics found that adolescents reporting symptoms of clinical depression increased by 37% between 2005 and 2014, and the suicide rate of youth aged 10–19 years rose by a devastating 56% between 2007 and 2016. Psychologist and author Jean M. Twenge wants you to believe that the "iGen," the generation shaped by smartphones and social media, born between 1995 and 2012, is "on the brink of the worst mental-health crisis in decades."

Much of this deterioration, she writes, can be traced to their phones. Twenge drew evidence from a nationwide study by the National Institute of Health, examining the relationship between screen time and psychological health among 40,000 children and adolescents in 2016. Twenge's and other surveys have found a link between the amount of screen time and mental issues like anxiety and depression, and conversely, a positive correlation between face-to-face interactions and a stronger sense of social well-being. It seems reasonable to believe that online interactions could lead to less healthy outcomes since more screen time implies less face-to-face time.

Twenge's hypothesis that depression is closely related to smartphones oversimplifies the problem. Peer competitiveness, academic loads, parental college goals, weight concerns, and relationship dynamics all play a role in shaping teenagers' behavior. There are far too many variables affecting the mental well-being of youth. Isolating smartphone use and social media as a significant

DOI: 10.4324/9781003453185-11

cause of declining mental health among teenagers minimizes other equally or even more relevant factors with the potential to socially alienate teens.

Social Norms and Future Generations

According to Arunas L. Radzvilaviciyou,[1] a postdoctoral researcher at the University of Pennsylvania, *"Teens who grow up in the age of smart phones and social media are statistically more likely to feel left out, lonely, and depressed. Social norms may be at play."*

It has become commonplace for media outlets to talk about this dark side of technology using the language of addiction. In a <u>Washington Post op-ed,</u> psychologist Doreen Dodgen-Magee called on mental health professionals to recognize the bleak reality of "tech addiction." In his <u>New York Times</u> column, Kevin Roose wrote about his "phone problem," and how it had broken his brain. Parents and teens often signal their unhappiness with the amount of time spent online by framing the issue as <u>smartphone addiction.</u>

> *"But to me, whereas addiction is something people experience mostly as individuals, social norms are shared mental states shaped by the views and beliefs of other members of the society and by our subjective perceptions of those beliefs. And I believe that with appropriate interventions, social norms can be swiftly and completely overturned."*

In the spirit of social media, here are some comments on the above post by Mr. Radzvilaviciyou. Names have been initialized to protect anonymity.

It is most definitely an addiction. As a parent of a teen, and a psychologist, I have been struggling to find a healthier way to integrate it into our lives. Every 'like', increases dopamine, and decreases patience and persistence. At best, communication and attention is reduced, and longer written work becomes laborious and uncreative. At worst, the 'type it as you feel it' catapults dramatic teen social interactions into intense bullying and suicidal ideation. Withdrawal occurs with irritability, moodiness, "boredom", struggles to tolerate less immediate stimuli, etc. Changing social norms are hard to do with constant steady hits of dopamine. -Dr. E.

The fact is, it is an addiction that has become socially acceptable by the majority, like smoking was in the 60's and 70's- very dangerous and unhealthy. Walk through a university campus and observe not one person (walking or driving) is paying attention with eyes forward, to watch where they're headed. I'm a psychology professor and addressing this issue on campus is an urgent priority. Two student pedestrians have been killed due to walking directly into oncoming traffic – sadly, video of one incident showed the individual failed to look up from their screen long enough to realize they were entering the roadway. Warning signs and vocal "STOP" lights have proved useless, as the students are so engrossed in thumb-typing, they ignore their surroundings. Long-term damage to the developing child's brain is real. It is a health crisis for you all. -J.K.

Addiction is not an individual disease but affects individuals on a biopsychosocial level. Entire families are disintegrating due to the over reliance on technology for communication. Individuals are obsessing over its use, it's interfering with their lives, they experience periods of withdrawal and are severely impacted. It certainly appears that there is a serious dependence which is having devastating effects on individuals, families and our entire society. While this does describe changes and social norms and also parallels the issues we're dealing currently with opiates and other substances creating dependence. I parallel this in my book, Turned On and Tuned Out: a Guide to Understanding and Managing Tech Dependence.

A Teen Responds to the Social Media Lie

Most social media users will abuse the privilege of communication and use it for something other than what is was intended to be. People developing a hedonistic and superficial lifestyle has led to the creation of the fake world of social media which is a means to portray oneself as the "perfect you." Rare is the post about a truly meaningful event, especially if it is a sad or makes one look imperfect... Because people subconsciously think their personality, this fake perfect life, is a reflection of what your life really is. People will take significant amounts out of every day of their lives to make sure to keep up this "perfect" world image. Studies show that the average person will spend two hours daily on social media. Excessive use of social media has been proven to cause higher rates of depression, anxiety, ad addiction on a major scale due to the fear of missing out on others "positive experiences...." One should always remember that just because it's in the virtual world, doesn't mean it won't affect the real one too.

–D.R. 17, Memphis, TN

Exercise:

How has social media affected your relationships with others? _____

How does social media affect your growth as a better person? _____

How does social media affect your self-worth? _____

What excuses and justifications do you use to convince yourself that it's OK to spend hours online? _____

Family Dysfunction

Freud: If it's not one thing, it's your mother—Robin Williams

Most family units do the best they can with the skills and history they have. No matter what, the child who lives in a dysfunctional system suffers from low self-esteem, codependency, trauma, abuse, and a lack of secure emotional attachment. These events cause children to become trapped in their own minds, constantly begging for attention and affection. When they don't receive the emotional nurturing they need, many turn to drugs, alcohol, sex, gambling, shopping, video games, etc.; anything to soothe the pain of internal loneliness.

Breach of Trust, Denial, and How to Rebuild It (Do We Need This Included?)

A great many people think they are thinking when they are merely rearranging their prejudices.— William James

A Letter from a concerned future spouse:

My problem is that I don't know what my opinion is. On one hand I understand that it's an addiction, and fight it as he might, it may just be too difficult for him to overcome now. But on the other hand, I can no longer tryout him when he says it's in the past. He claims that it's not an addiction and that since discussing it with me this second time and realizing how much it hurts me, he feels 100% confident that it won't happen again. I've tried to convince him to join a support group but he claims that he knows of these things and they won't help him.

My response:

This is all his addiction talking. Step one is the admission he is powerless over this. He is nowhere near that stage. Knowing it is hurting you won't stop it from happening again. Give him a few weeks and let's see. Support groups like AA, NA, SLAA, SA, OA are the medicine for helping people overcome denial and begin the path to recovery.

She continues…

Finally, we agreed that together we would go to a relationship counselor to try to work this out. He seems bothered by the notion that if he had proposed to me a night earlier, I would have said yes, but now I'm not as definite. Today, a couple of days later, he seems to be largely in a cloud of depression, and it hurts me to see him that way. I want to help him, and the only way I know how is to help him get help, but all he's willing to do is go to a relationship counselor for one session and is convinced that I'll leave that session feeling confident that he's better. I'm not so confident, and I wish he weren't either.

I understand that recovery is not achieved over the course of a second, and I'm willing to stand by him as long as he makes the effort, but he doesn't seem to be. Now any time the topic is raised he gets all agitated with me, telling me that he should never have told me in the first place (even though I have told him repeatedly that his honesty means the world to me).

I grew up with a verbally abusive father and am very sensitive to put-downs. I'm starting to view his curtness as a forerunner to verbal abuse. I'm reaching the end of my rope and I don't know what to do. I understand that it's different in a situation where the man is married with kids, but my situation is very different. I love this man and I want to marry him, but is it a mistake rushing ahead to get engaged as we were about to without first and foremost resolving this problem? Depending on how serious an addiction he has (assuming he does have one of some sort), it could take years for him to fully recover, and neither one of you is willing to push off marriage that long. Is it stupid of me to marry someone who I know has had this problem and claims that it's in the past?

My response:

YES. Until he has committed to individual and group therapy and can prove his sobriety for at least 90 days, if you're asking me, I would not get engaged and then face the disaster to break it off. Please don't do that to yourself or your friend. You're too good a person. I can tell.

About your father: You've just hit the nail on the head. If your man is curt, and in your gut, you feel it's the forerunner for verbal abuse, you're setting yourself up for a reenactment of how your father treated you. If you've been verbally abused, he is picking you up because you are setting yourself up to be codependent of him. He'll act out, you love him so you'll hope and wish he won't do it again, he'll apologize and say things like, "we'll if it were last night we would be engaged." He's probably experienced trauma in some way also. People with this addiction have very low self-esteem and they medicate themselves with porn, chat rooms, dating sites, alcohol, drugs, sex, gambling, etc. In recovery, he will begin to face this and explore ways to feel better about himself.

I'm so torn over this. Part of me knows that I'll probably never find anyone as open and honest as he is, and knowing the nature of men, if I were to marry anyone else, there's a good chance that he'll also have a problem of this nature and even worse he may be trying to hide it from me.

What are you basing this global, mind-reading thinking on? Every man does not have this problem. Honesty is great, but if there is no desire to get better, it is meaningless. He is just setting you up to get married and then controlling you. He thinks that when he marries you, the slavery of addiction will simply fade away. Unfortunately, in my experience that is not the case, because it's not about the partner. It's about what is the trigger driving the addict to continue to act out.

Why We Allow Other People to Annoy Us?

When confusion grips a person's soul he is locked in solitude, drifting away from people, lost in his own little world, running away from life itself. Part of the obsession of expecting others to do what we think they should do, our way, is hyper-vigilance; thinking everyone must believe and act the way we think they should. The point is that people are influenced by their surroundings and when you're around people who are apathetic toward taking action; you become apathetic and believe you're seeing others for who they really are according to your personal definition. We allow people to annoy us because we're not happy with ourselves. We can put on a mask all day for the outer world to see while living a life of anger, frustration, restlessness, and irritability.

As a client once said,

My life is still full of doubts, lost dreams and expectations, illness and sadness grip my soul. Is it punishment or coincidence? Why bother when I'm miserable no matter what I do. This eternal question still haunts me. Another year of struggle and triumph, illness and health, death and birth. Life continues in all its misery and we coast along apathetically year after year until we're buried, with nothing to show for this life of hypocrisy and apathy, of masking our true feelings so others will think of you as we think of ourselves, not willing to change.

Why harp on the faults of others when we have no control or ability to stop them? Yet we are to radically accept despite our own rights and needs for a voice for ourselves. Do we ignore what we need because other people control our destiny? When we are stuck, banging our heads against several walls at one, trying to figure out how the puzzle of life fits together.

These comments bring home the fact that when we allow other people to affect our emotions, we're setting ourselves up for a life of desperation, depression, and despondency.

Judging and comparing are our worst enemies. Judging others and comparing ourselves to others leads to feelings of depression, fear, guilt, shame, rejection, and jealousy. Judging ourselves compared to others leads to emptiness, insecurity, apathy, and dependency. What gives you peace of mind is a high level of self-respect that leads to self-esteem. When we feel worthy of ourselves, it doesn't matter what other people think or do. We enjoy a feeling of confidence, fulfillment, joy, tryout, purpose, and integrity. To achieve a level of acceptance and forgiveness for others and for ourselves, we need faith, hope, love, and total unconditional acceptance, not just lip service.

What gets in the way of our acceptance is that we think if we accept our past, we are condoning it and saying it was OK. Actually, that is not the case. We cannot change the past and when we continue to hold on to it and not accept it as reality, we are allowing the perpetrators of our trauma to live rent-free in our minds forever and ever. The point is not to forget and let go, moving forward working toward a life worth living.

Radical Acceptance

Acceptance is all about what you have control over and what you don't and knowing the difference. It's a method for coping under stress. Radical acceptance is learning to be skillful enough to let things go, like your past, that you cannot change and move forward. It is not about approval or resignation. You don't have to like what happened in your past, but you also need to move forward in your life. It's the fundamental principle of Dialectical Behavior Therapy; we accept people or situations the way they are and know that there is room for improvement.

In order to accept your life, you have to accept reality as it is. Remember:

- Reality is what it is (even if you hate it).
- Everything happens for a reason (even if you don't know why).
- Everything is as it should be. You are where you should be doing what you should be doing at this time.

Non-Judgmental Stance

No person in the world can be totally non-judgmental. It's human nature to make judgments and decisions based on what we see and hear. The issue with being judgmental is, it causes the emotional part of your mind to increase in intensity. Usually, when you judge someone else through an emotional lens, rather than a logical one, your emotion, and judgment will usually be negative.

Here's how to become less judgmental:

a. First, your attitude determines your altitude and to the degree that you are aware of being less judgmental, you will succeed.

b. Second, increase your awareness with your judging. During the day become aware of your feelings and when you're feeling less than glorious, be careful not to be judgmental of others. Also don't be judgmental of yourself.

c. Third, once you catch yourself judging, accept it, instead of putting yourself down. In other words, "don't judge yourself for judging."

Adapted from Marsha Linehan's Skills Training Manual for Treating Borderline Personality Disorder, Guilford Press, 1993.

Exercise:

Is your past or present causing you to suffer? _____

Do you feel like you're stuck and can't move on? _____

How difficult is it for you to accept where you are in life? _____

What is stopping you from accepting your own reality? _____

Who are you allowing to direct your life without your permission? _____

What annoys you most about people in general? _____

If I let the past go, that means _____.

The benefit I get from holding on to my past is _____.

The benefit I get from constantly worrying about the future is? (Think in terms of needing to be in control).

_____

What types of things are you most judgmental about? _____

List three things, people, situations, beliefs that you can let go of judgment and accept as is.

_____
_____
_____

Adapted from Marsha Linehan's Skills Training Manual for Treating Borderline Personality Disorder, Guilford Press, 1993.

Resentments

Holding on to resentments is like drinking poison and hoping the other person will die. This age-old expression sums up the futility of holding on to resentments. One of the pathways to happiness is doing good deeds for other people. It makes you happy to help those in need. The problem leads to resentment when we have expectations of other people that they will reciprocate. When they don't appreciate what we do for them, or make unusual demands upon our time and efforts, we build resentment. Other people hold on to resentments from their past and cannot move forward in life.

Leading a Double Life

A truly spiritual person cannot lead a double life. Some of you escaped the hell of a fractured home relationship and live a double life. Scared to speak up, feeling lonely and abandoned emotionally, we think we must escape because feelings were blowing in the wind. No one would listen. Severe anxiety weakens our happiness. The chemicals in our brain, starving for connection, take over, and erase any semblance of happy feelings. The saddest thing is even in old age we allow idiots to intimidate you. Enabling and caretaking take the place of simply caring and doing for others. Being a crass, obnoxious person has become normal and selfish and glorified as "healthy."

No one ends up a priority when a person leads a double life of portraying themselves on the outside as a seriously spiritual person but on the inside doesn't truly believe in anything but themselves and their narrow-minded opinion that the only thing that matters in the world is them!

Turning Envy into a Positive Character Trait

People annoy you because sometimes we see ourselves in them. We are critical of others and what we criticize is a character flaw in ourselves we need to change. It's easier to find fault in others than to examine and change yourself. Envy, or comparing ourselves to others and wishing we were more like them, causes you to be critical of others because we feel we fall short of our own expectations. But envy can be turned into a positive trait.

In Path of the Just, Gate of Humility it states,

> They asked one of the pious ones – How did you become a master of all the generations? He answered, because when I saw someone, I assumed he was greater. If they were wiser, I said they have more awe of Heaven. If they were not as wise, I said, they are guilty of oversight, but my sins are purposeful. If they are older than I, I said, their merits are greater than mine. If I am older, I said, their faults are less than mine. And if we are equal in age, I said that their heart is greater than mine. If they are richer than I, I said that they have given more charity, and if they are poorer than I, I said they are humbler and better than me. And for these reasons, I would honor them, and be deferential toward them.

When you can look at others in this way, you can begin to make yourself and others close to you a priority, by humbling yourself to the reality that no one is perfect, not even you.

Exercise:

What benefit do you get from holding on to resentments? _____

What was your part in why you continue to hold on? _____

Why do you find it difficult to tryout others? _____

When you compare yourself to others, what are you saying about yourself? _____

_____

What benefit do you get from judging yourself negatively? (*There is no benefit* is not an acceptable answer. You wouldn't do it if there were no benefits!) _____

_____

How can you build tryout back into your personal relationship? _____

What form of technology or work do you need to cut back on to make your family a priority?

_____

How does humility play a role in your remaining controlled by other people?_____

_____

Note

1 Arunas L. Radzvilaviciyou is a postdoctoral researcher at the University of Pennsylvania and a research fellow at the Institute for Advanced Study in Berlin. He currently works on theoretical models of human behavior, evolution of social norms, and moral emotions. (Undark.com).

Chapter 8

The Solution of Safety and Trust

Duties of the Heart states: *Trust the tranquility of the soul, a healthy reliance on the one whom he trusts, and the latter will do what is proper in the matter of the tryout, to the extent of his ability and knowledge, for the benefit of the one who trusts... The essence of his truthfulness is his sure confidence that the person he trusts will fulfill what he promised and execute what he pledges to do, and, even where there is no promise, has in mind to benefit the one who trusts him, and all out of benevolence and kindness.*

Trusting a Higher Power

My self-worth is defined by walking my walk, talking my talk, fidelity and respecting myself, a Higher Power and other people, by doing what I say I'm going to do, when I say I'm going to do it.

Trust is the number one-character trait where all others are intertwined. When you have faith, there is no need to get angry, scared, or depressed. Accepting where you are in life is where you are supposed to be, is the path to serenity. Living in the present moment, not reliving your past or worrying about your future, is the path to emotional sobriety, peace of mind, and freedom. When you tryout in a Higher Power, you will become independent, not needing to place hope in another person or in yourself. You will not have to please other people to make them like you or have to flatter them to please you. You will be free to express yourself because you don't have to depend on them for your self-worth.

In the words of Duties of the Heart, *if one trusts in God, his soul is at rest, his heart tranquil, untroubled by decrees.... But one who does not trusts in God, even when he is prosperous, he is always troubled and in a state of continual anxiety, mourning and grieving (because of his lust) to increase and multiply his possessions and hoard them.*

According to Abraham Amsel in Judaism and Psychology (84, Feldheim, NY, 1969), "*trust presupposes the belief that God molds circumstances in accordance with His will, that He wills the good of man and that He is completely just in His reward and punishment, the latter attribute, presupposes the free will of man.*"

People who openly deny the existence of God and therefore cannot put their trust in a Higher Power greater than themselves, cannot enjoy genuine peace of mind, tranquility, and contentment. They are crippled by fears and anxiety because they have no real power to hold onto for security. They hold on to the belief that they can control themselves and don't need

DOI: 10.4324/9781003453185-12

anyone to give them help or a crutch to push forward. They become the gods of their own understanding.

Imagine, if you were given the task of forming a living planet with trees, fruits, vegetables, humans, and animals. Use your imagination and figure out what new types of fruits and vegetables could you create. What would they look like, smell like, taste like? Then imagine you were the Higher Power and you could create and do whatever you wanted. Of course, you would be an all-loving god because that's what we all want to envision. Anything and everything is permitted in your society. There are no laws, rules, decrees, customs, consequences, or punishments. No natural disasters, just everyone does as they please until someone gets upset at someone else and kills them, or runs a red light, wrecks a car, or someone falls from a three-story building and injures themselves. Now what are you going to do? Just say, *oh well, you can do whatever you want to whomever you want and there are no consequences?* What kind of world would that be? Then make sure the sun rises in the morning and sets in the evening and you'll have to create seasons so the vegetables and fruit you create can grow. Or, you could just go on perpetual vacation and let the chips fall where they may. How long do you think this society would last?

Trust in God does not mean standing around in busy traffic and getting run over, or sitting on your porch all day, hoping someone will shower down money upon your household. No. You still have to put in the effort to work and put food on your table. The extent of abundance is out of your control. You have to put in the work and tryout God with the results. Otherwise, constant worry will never bring peace of mind and tranquility of spirit. A person who tryouts God does not get upset when his requests are not granted. Do you ever tell your children NO? Then why is it so difficult for you to accept no from a Higher Power who has your best interest at heart?

How Am I Supposed to Have Trust If I Grew Up with Abuse and Trauma?

People have free will to do as they please, and therefore we cannot blame God for what people do to others. We find people in society who are willing to suffer for the greater good of society, like firefighters, doctors, and soldiers. But sometimes people suffer against their will and it could be for the sake of keeping free will present in society. If every time someone decided to do evil and God prevented it, there would be no free choice.

A person might ask, why me? And that's a question that cannot be answered with any form of certainty. God gives you many tests in life, some of which we understand and some of which we cannot. You are alive today, despite the abuse and trauma. You are a survivor, not a victim any longer. Your task in life from now on is to heal from past trauma and abuse and move forward in breaking the generational chain that has so captivated your mind.

According to Rabbi Shmuel Waldman in *"Beyond A Reasonable Doubt," Sorrow possesses great potential power to expand our lives, enlarge our vision, and deepen our understanding. Grief can also help purge you of immature pettiness and selfishness.* It can build our strength back with patience and a new understanding of human nature.

A client writes, *"Bankruptcy literally and emotionally has been a recurring theme in my life. Addiction comes along and makes it worse, a roller coaster over and over the same bumps and hills. I have no regrets."*

Trusting Other People

Keith Ayers of Integro Leadership developed the concept of four Elements of Trust. Other people annoy you often because we're projecting our own insecurities onto them. Or we're so stressed out, everything and everybody emotionally gets in the way. Developing tryout in others is difficult when we've had past experiences of abuse and trauma, betrayal or other breaches of tryout. Keeping our word helps other people trust you and in turn we feel better about ourselves and begin to trust others. Once we trust others and give people the benefit of the doubt, we become less annoyed and more accepting of other people.

Reliability: I will do what I say when I say I will do it. This is one of the things that annoys you about other people. Not doing what they say they are going to do when they say they will do it.
Openness: I will share information with you that will help you do a better job. I will ask for feedback from you so I can do a better job.
Acceptance: Who you are is OK with me. I may disagree with you, but you are still a valuable person to me.
Congruence: I will walk my walk and talk my talk. I will mean what I say and say what I mean.

We hide what we know or feel ourselves to be (which we assume to be unacceptable and unlovable) behind some kind of appearance which we hope will be more pleasing. We hide behind pretty faces which we put on for the benefit of our public. And in time we may even come to forget that we are hiding, and think that our assumed pretty faces is what we really look like.

(Simon Tugwell, The Beatitudes: Soundings in Christian Traditions)

Trusting Yourself

The ultimate question is how to react to other people, to affect you in a positive, rather than negative way. The balance point is acceptance on one hand and being so comfortable with yourself on the other, that the thought of resentment does not even enter your mind.

The question is, "how do we achieve this level of trusting ourselves?"

When the mind wanders into someone else's emotional space and the heart wants a one-way connection, it's time to live your own life, not through others' lenses but through your own cherished uniqueness. Anything else is a recipe for disappointment.

When our expectations of others' sincerity are measured by our own biased low expectations of ourselves; when we cannot validate our own specialness because we're waiting for others to do it for us, we spend our lives existing in the shadowy expectations of others without regard for what makes you unique, fulfilled, and ultimately happy.

We alone must nourish our inner child, not on the whims of other's hectic lifestyles, but on the values, beliefs, and traditions that have molded our benevolent actions thus far. We cannot dictate how others care for you. We can only dictate acceptance of ourselves and accepting others for what they do. And if inactions speak louder than words then we listen and next time, accept their intentions as upright and their inactions as simple human weakness.

We all strive in our hearts to love and be loved by others, but one cannot dictate how someone loves you, only how we show and experience love for others. Only when we love ourselves can we accept other's love in the way <u>they</u> feel like expressing it, not by our own expectant standards of heightening our own self-worth through the actions of others.

Why Are You Not Making Me a Priority?

Every day clients tell me their main complaint in their relationship is they don't feel like a priority. Work schedules, technological distractions, raising children, and the monotony of routine, isolate couples into a fantasy existence where all they want to do is escape and forget about life. But when we live in fantasy, we cannot make another person a priority. And we will accomplish nothing. Rest is important, but spending your entire day, sitting on your couch watching TV or playing video games on your phone is simply a waste of time. You're not even making your potential a priority; let alone someone you love. When we work and play together, with goals and dreams to look forward to, we can accomplish anything. But when you have nothing to look forward to, you spend your life wandering around the forest, looking for a way out; ignoring the one person in your life who craves love, connection, and intimacy.

We don't make others a priority because we've never learned how to have a secure attachment with another human being. People who grow up emotionally abandoned don't know how to have a healthy, close connection with another person. The fear of rejection is so great, it shuts down any semblance of closeness or safety; trusting another human being with our skeletons in the closet.

Becoming Honest with Ourselves

What we resist persists. When we overwhelm ourselves and tell ourselves we have to be clean for 90 days, it puts a lot of pressure on us. And if we also have a fear of failure, it's a sure sign we will act out. By giving yourself permission and accepting reality, you take the wind out of the sails of the addiction.

I received a private email from a 17-year-old living at home. He had put hundreds of dollars on his parent's credit card talking on a chat line. He was overseas at the time and when he got home his parents asked him about it. He told them he knew nothing about it.

He wrote asking me if he should continue to lie or tell his parents the truth. I told him that life was short and if he truly wanted to learn what honesty is, and start his life off right, he couldn't live a lie the rest of his life. I told him exactly how to tell his parents the truth. He wrote to me and said he told his parents, and they were very happy he did. If you had a serious illness, would you hide it from your parents?

Being honest with yourself means to stop rationalizing and making excuses why you can continue to tread along the edge of disaster. What would happen if you went out of town or on vacation and didn't take your computer? Do you think you'd live through it? People have lived for thousands of years without computers and smartphones. When you earn your livelihood on a computer, you can place safeguards and accountability software to protect yourself. But if you don't work on a computer all day, there is really no excuse to spend every free minute for the rest of your life looking at your phone or a computer screen. This is what it means… going to any length to get and stay sober.

Forgiveness and Acceptance

Thinking we deserve to stay miserable enshrouded in guilt and shame for our past actions is irrelevant. Forgiveness is necessary to move forward in a new way. Ask yourself what holding on to your guilt and shame does for you? What benefit do you get from holding on to past traumas, abuse, and irrational decisions? What has holding on to these things caused in your past? Can this be the reason you don't feel like a priority?

> Forgiveness is not absolution; it is a form of self-acceptance. At its core, forgiveness is not, in fact, about the other person. It's about you, and what we believe we need in order to move through a reckoning of the self. No one has the power to deliver you from our past mistakes. Only we can forgive ourselves by coming to terms with what we're holding onto.
>
> (Leigh Huggins, http://leighhuggins.com)

Brene Brown says in *Rising Strong*,

> 'In order for forgiveness to happen, something has to die. If you make a choice to forgive, you have to face the pain. You simply have to hurt…' The death or ending that forgiveness necessitates comes in many shapes and forms. We may need to bury our expectations or dreams. We may need to relinquish the power that comes with 'being right' or put to rest the idea that we can do what's in our hearts and still retain the support or approval of others…So, forgiveness is not forgetting or walking away from accountability or condoning a hurtful act; it's the process of taking back and healing our lives so we can truly live.

Forgiveness is necessary to heal and to change the direction of our lives. Forgiveness does not mean acceptance. Forgive but do not forget and stop allowing the past to rent space in your brain any longer.

You will find yourself judging yourself and others from time to time. Simply turn your mind away from these judgmental thoughts and toward how you can use this interaction in a more positive way; perhaps giving the person the benefit of the doubt! Turn away from judgmental thinking and begin to focus on what is possible to achieve today.

Rebuilding Trust

Assumptions are the termites of a relationship

To rebuild trust an addict must train himself to show compassion, love, empathy, intimacy, and romance in other ways besides being sexual. Your partner might think sex is all you think about, so if you can show her you have no such expectations when you show affection, she will begin to feel safe around you.

Work together on other ways to feel close. Don't wait for her to tell you to take out the garbage or wash the dishes or help with the kids. Take charge of doing what's right. Your job from now on is to do and say nice things for your partner, whether she reciprocates or not. When you do this, things will change. It may take a few months or a year, but your intimacy will be richer both in the bedroom and out.

The key is to set aside times to talk to your partner. Our partners feel less of a priority because we isolate and distract ourselves and ignore them. Your partner can be your biggest fan and help in all these matters, when you become vulnerable enough to let her in and discover the real you, with all your warts and foibles. Tell her you get very frustrated when you really need to talk. It's not easy. Changing ourselves is never easy and that's why we have to talk about it to heal.

A partner cannot expect you to be totally 100% impulse-free. It is impossible and will cause undue stress. Unless you want to live as a hermit in a cave, you and your wife will have to learn to live in the outside world. A wise counselor once told me it is natural to be attracted to the opposite sex, and as long as you are doing nothing about it, there is nothing wrong with it. You cannot be expected to walk in the street with your head constantly between your legs because you might bump into a fire hydrant.

Exercise:

Write brief sentences beginning with the following words:

If I forgive it means_____

I can never forgive myself because _____

Even if I forgive eventually, I will never forget because_____

I will rebuild tryout with my partner by _____

I understand that acceptance is the key to an emotionally healthy life because_____

_____

In my relationship, I can make myself a priority by_____

_____

In my relationship, I can make my partner a priority by….

_____

_____

Section V

Sexuality and Intimacy

Chapter 9

The Intensity of Unhealthy Sexual Behavior

Laurell K. Hamilton wrote, *"Only love of a good woman will make a man question every choice, every action. Only love makes a warrior hesitate for fear that his lady will find him cruel. Only love makes a man both the best he will ever be, and the weakest. Sometimes all in the same moment."*

A major stumbling block on the journey to freedom begins in the bedroom. Work, distractions, people, and emotions block you from feeling like a priority in your relationships, and this affects how you experience sexuality and intimacy. The problem is when you seek out sex when you need nurturing; it's like being hungry and putting on one coat after another. You're hot but you're still hungry!

Men and women have different templates about sex. Some women link sex with their feelings during the day. They get many of their emotional needs met elsewhere like talks with their friends. On the other hand, men who don't understand healthy sexuality come home from work tired, grumpy, stressed out, and sad and want to have sex to feel better. Yet when their partner sees they are moody and irritable, they don't want to have anything to do with them. Men take this as a personal rejection, doubting themselves, and their partner's love for them.

Some men subconsciously sexualize and objectify women, including wives and partners, thanks to the underlying messages drilled into them through the media and entertainment industry. These men want to feel connected to the women in their lives. They want to feel close, loved, and respected. They want to matter, to be a priority. They want to feel heard. And they mistakenly believe that objectifying their partners is the way to accomplish that and fill those needs. At the same time, women also want to feel connected and safe intimately in other ways outside the bedroom. Safety is their priority. But when they feel objectified and sexualized, the result is the exact opposite: They feel unsafe and unprotected.

Sex is a spiritual bond between two people, a mutual understanding that this is <u>one</u> way to show their love for one another. Yet, both must feel safe and vulnerable enough to experience real intimacy. If your partner senses you are full of lust and just want to have sex for your <u>own</u> physical desires, they will resist, or worse, give in, and resent you.

Healthy sexuality is about mutual consent rather than manipulation and intimidation. It's about not exploiting your partner's weaknesses and insecurities about body image, nor their past traumas that may trigger fear or flashbacks. It's about honesty, shared values, and mutual pleasure (Braun-Harvey & Vigorito, 2015).

DOI: 10.4324/9781003453185-14

Healthy sexuality	Unhealthy sexuality
Each person is accepting and comfortable with their body	One or both partners feel uncomfortable, shame, or critical of their body
Affection without expectations of making love	Affection is expressed only for the goal of having sex
Freedom to choose where each partner has a choice	Sex as an expectation, pressure, manipulation, guilted
Healthy boundaries, safety, and sexual mastery	Unrestrained, disrespected boundaries, obsessive, compulsive actions
Sex based on mutual connection focused on each other	Sex based on performance and outcome
Both partners are physically, mentally, and emotionally engaged and present	One or both partners are mentally and emotionally detached, or fantasizing about others
Healthy communication about thoughts and beliefs	Ignoring the other's feelings and desires, degrading, harm
Mutually agreeable variety, novelty, fun, and adventure	Forced or pressured variety and novelty
Mutually fulfilling desired outcome for both partners	Self-gratifying results in partners resentment toward sex
Open, honest, and transparent to see and be seen	Secretive, hidden
Spontaneous expression of mutual, nurturing love	Obsessive focus on sex compulsively

Sexual Compulsivity and Love Addiction

The chemicals involved in chemical addiction, such as dopamine and serotonin, are also involved in sexual compulsivity. Let's say you are walking on the beach. You see an attractive person. If you're attracted to that other person, you are having a mood-altering event. These good feelings are the result of the release of pleasurable brain chemicals, or neurotransmitters. You are in some degree of sexual stimulation. This is nothing new or pathological.

Compulsivity on a psychological level begins when we become attached to the <u>feelings</u> associated with our sexual practices and we create a primary relationship with those feelings. Sex becomes more important than the person we have sex with. Addiction develops when our feelings associated with the activity, rather than the person, become our main source of comfort, filling up a void in our soul to relieve feelings of loneliness and boredom.

The love addict begins to confuse these feelings with love and life and loses other ways of relieving loneliness and boredom or feeling good. If someone becomes too attracted to these feelings and sensations, they begin to confuse intensity with intimacy. They believe that sexual excitement (lust) that brings on these feelings is the source of love and joy, which they cannot live without. The brain gets used to functioning on these higher levels of neurotransmitters, constantly requiring more stimulation, novelty, danger, or excitement. The body, however, cannot sustain such intensity and it begins to shut down parts of the brain that receive these chemicals. Tolerance develops and the sex addict begins to need more and more sexual excitement to get back the feelings of joy and happiness.

Sex addiction is not about sex. Howard Shaffer, associate professor of psychiatry and director of the Division on Addictions at Harvard Medical School, said, *"The idea of addictive drugs makes no sense, it's magical thinking to imagine that drugs have this power. We don't talk about addictive dice."* (cited in Lambert, 2000). However, we do know that for some individuals their relationship to dice can become pathological. The focus needs to shift away from the dice back to the individual holding them. It is the relationship between the person and the object of addiction that matters, not the objects. The denial of the existence of addiction is not new. Compulsive behaviors have historically been attributed to a person's moral deficiencies, weakness in character and negative personality traits.

As more and more addicts' energy becomes focused on relationships that have sexual potential, other relationships and activities—family, friends, work, talents, and values—suffer and atrophy from neglect. Long-term relationships are stormy and often unsuccessful. Because of sexual overextension and intimacy avoidance, short-term relationships become the norm. Sometimes, however, the desire to preserve an important long-term relationship with spouse or children, for instance, can act as the catalyst for addicts to admit their problem and seek help.

The Avoidance of Normal Intimate Relationships

In sex and love addiction, a parallel situation exists. Sex—like food, drugs, or gambling—provides the "high" and addicts become dependent on this sexual high to feel normal. They substitute healthy relationships for unhealthy ones. They opt for temporary pleasure rather than the deeper qualities of "normal" intimate relationships.

Sex and love addicts struggle to control their behaviors, and experience despair over their constant failure to do so. Their loss of self-esteem grows, fueling the need to escape even further into their addictive behaviors. A sense of powerlessness pervades the lives of addicts. They feel tremendous guilt and shame about their out-of-control behavior, and they live in constant fear of discovery. Yet addicts will often act out sexually to block out the very pain of their addiction. This is part of what drives the addictive cycle. Like other forms of addiction, sex addicts are out of control and unable to stop their behaviors despite their self-destructive nature and potentially devastating consequences.

Empathy and Intimacy after Trauma

Laura Dawn Lewis (above) coined the concept of the Eight Stages of Intimacy. One of the eight stages is emotional intimacy, which covers feelings, tryout, security, and safety in a relationship. Many couples never achieve emotional intimacy because you have to accept your partner for who he or she is without reservation. At this level of intimacy, the couple feels comfortable sharing anger, happiness, secrets, sensual and sexual feelings. Each of you knows you are loved and loves your partner, no matter how either of you feels or acts.

When betrayal, abuse, infidelity, or trauma occur, the wounds run so deep that emotional intimacy is diminished, and it becomes difficult for the wounded partner to feel comfortable enough to share anger, happiness, and other feelings. Some spouses call for a cooling-off period of celibacy so the addict can heal the damage to the brain and don't feel safe enough to engage in intimate activity until they can tryout their partner once again.

To build intimacy and empathy, the wounded partner needs to know that the addict understands the pain is due to the addict's poor choices and not the wounded partner's fault. Emotional intimacy is achieved when tryout is established again, and the couple can speak about sensitive topics without constantly bringing up past indiscretions.

Here are some examples of how to build intimacy with empathy:

1. In a state of fear, uncertainty, or danger, your partner is the person you turn to for comfort.
2. Crying, showing frustration, sadness, or anger in front of your partner is healthy. You know he/she will not see you as weak, psychotic, crazy, or out of control.
3. You can speak about sex, secrets, and your feelings without a fear of being betrayed, ridiculed, or compromised.
4. No matter what happens, you know your partner loves you and will not abandon you during a state of crisis, ill health, or financial difficulty.
5. You show or tell each other often, through words and actions, that you love and respect each other.
6. Past wrongs are not dredged up in arguments to get even with each other. The past is discussed, forgiven, and left there. This may take some time recovering from betrayal, but when both partners work on healing themselves, the chances of recapturing the intimacy can be achieved through empathy for each other.
7. Passive aggressive behavior and name-calling do not exist in your relationship.

Questions to Determine Emotional Intimacy

TO THE BETRAYED PARTNER: What will it take for you to feel safe in this relationship?

_____

_____

TO THE ADDICT: What will it take for you to want to build tryout within this relationship?

_____

Can you show empathy when your partner respects and admires you, or would you prefer that your partner listen to your feelings and cherish you?

_____

_____

Have you ever cried in front of your partner? If not, what is your fear about being this vulnerable? What's the worst that can happen? Has that ever happened? If yes, did your partner react with empathy or with scorn?

_____

_____

_____

_____

Chapter 10

The Intimacy of Healthy Sexual Behavior

The Key to Understanding Sex and Love Addiction

The key to understanding the loss of control in addicts is the concept of the "hijacked brain." Addicts essentially have rewired their brains so that they do behaviors (drinking, drug use, eating, gambling, and sex) even when they are intending to do something quite different. The triggers to these maladaptive responses are usually stress, emotional pain, loneliness, abandonment, or specific childhood scenarios of sexual abuse or sexual trauma. Breakthrough science in examining brain function is helping you to understand the biology of this disease.

The remedy is, as the SLAA book says, "*The crucial change in attitude came when we admitted we were powerless over our addiction, and we withdrew from our habit. For some it meant no sex with themselves or others, including getting into relationships. For others it meant "drying out" and not having sex with their spouse for a time to recover from lust.*

Lust and Desire

The White Book of Sexaholics Anonymous describes lust as not being sexual or physical. It's a "screen of self-indulgent fantasy separating me from reality." When lust is driving my bus, sex with my spouse becomes fantasy instead of true intimacy. Lust creates a desire for more, no matter what the other person wants or feels. It's a selfish preoccupation with my own desires, not taking the other person's feelings into consideration. "It's a force that infuses and distorts my other instincts as well: eating, drinking, working, and anger."

I had a counselor once tell me that it was OK to fantasize as long as you don't act on the fantasy. If you're an addict, lust is a cunning and baffling "devil" that can make you do things we swore we would never do. It really boils down to the fact that you cannot control your thoughts. Thinking is not a sin. The trick is to accept the thoughts and let them go, think about something else. Sometimes people think they have to do something when they have a thought or feeling. You really don't. Instead, let the thought go or wait for the feeling to pass and distract yourself with something else. If you want to live a life of spirituality and congruency, be honest with yourself and spend your time on more noble activities other than video games and social media.

However, when you find yourself on the computer for hours at a time and you can't stop until you get another "fix" of inappropriate videos, then you have an addiction problem, no matter what you're acting out with or whom. The only thing your thoughts damage is your soul. When we're living a life of congruity with our values, when we're living in the present moment and not lusting for the future or reliving the abuses of the past, then we're living a serene life, spiritually, psychologically, and socially.

DOI: 10.4324/9781003453185-15

Once a person begins to realize that sex is not the most important aspect of his life and it is indeed optional, your private relationship will improve tremendously.

Dov, a recovering addict with over 26 years of sobriety, shares his unique perspective on how to live a sober life.

The traditional AA approach saved my life. By this I mean the AA message that I have a mental illness of addiction to lust, a spiritual disconnect from God and people, and a physical allergy to lust, that will eventually kill me. Immoral lusting in any way makes my life completely unmanageable and makes me useless to others. Many other people appear to be able to use it a little without suffering as I do. For them it is just a 'moral failing' while for me it leads to a downward spiral of insanity and failure, just like alcohol for an alcoholic. *The message was to accept the fact that I am fundamentally different from non-addicts and accept that I am not a bad person getting good, but rather a sick person getting well – with help from my Higher Power. I had to accept that this disease had me completely beaten, just like cancer or diabetes. You don't struggle against a disease, you get treatment.* Plenty of people don't and they die as a result.

I never got better until I saw the extent and quality of my acting out was indeed ill. The spiritual approach of religion was not working because I wasn't trying hard enough, but rather there was something wrong with my approach. In the 12-step groups I discovered the following:

1. *As long as I looked at myself as "I am a regular, healthy guy on the whole, but sadly have this terrible habit – I'd never get better."*
2. *As long as I remained absolutely disgusted with myself, I'd never get better. We are not "bad" people who need to become "good," but simply "ill" people who need to get "better."*

Dov continues, *I believe I was really serving lust. I depended on it, it took up my entire mind so often, I did it in private and I protected my access to it be keeping it safe and secret – because even though I hated myself so much for it, I desperately feared losing it. Just try to force an addict to quit and see how long it takes him to feel absolutely desperate – after the bravado of "sure, I can go without it" is over and done with.*

The Eight Stages of Intimacy:©

1. **Physical Intimacy:** Looks, etiquette, and charisma. Something you like about the person. It also includes cuddling, holding hands, and sensual touch.
2. **Aesthetic Intimacy:** Arts, style, culture, and general compatibility. Having common interests.
3. **Recreational Intimacy:** Shared interests, sports and hobbies, games, and recreation. Love spending time together and doing activities together. You do not get upset if your partner spends time without you pursuing their own interests. It also includes sharing routines instead of keeping score, trying new things together, consistency, adventure, and spontaneity.
4. **Intellectual Intimacy:** Hopes, fears, opinions, and beliefs are shared and discussed. It also includes having deep conversations about things that matter in your relationship, mental stimulation, curiosity, and creativity.

5. **Spiritual Intimacy:** Morality, ethics, and shared goals. It also includes prayer, meditation, faith, tryout in a higher power, and shared values.
6. **Emotional Intimacy:** Feelings, tryout, security, and safety. Who do you call first? It also includes empathy, respect, validation, communication, and vulnerability.
7. **Sexual Intimacy:** Touching, romance, intercourse, and procreation. The right to accept or decline without fear of ridicule, rape, or coercion. Or withholding sex as a tool of manipulation.
8. **Unconditional Love:** Love and support without strings attached, expectations, or regrets. No matter what someone does, says, or is, you love them fully and without reservation or expecting anything in return.

Exercise: FANOS

FANOS is a simple five-step check-in exercise. It is meant to be completed daily and briefly, 5–10 minutes or less per check-in, with no feedback or comments given from the listener. If further discussion is desired, it can take place after both parties have presented their check-in. This exercise involves both parties sharing. The couple should decide in advance on a regular time for this exercise.

The outline for the check-in is as follows:

- F – Feelings – What are you feeling emotionally right now (focus on primary feelings instead of secondary feelings). Avoid talking about your feelings toward the relationship. Rather, feelings that have come up during the day.

  This exercise is designed to help you communicate better and to build intimacy, not to create additional conflict.
- A – Affirmation – Share something specific you appreciate that your partner did since the last check-in.
- N – Need – What are your current needs.
- O – Ownership – Admit something that you did since the last check-in that was not helpful in your relationship.
- S – Sobriety – State if you have or have not maintained sobriety since the last check-in. The definition of sobriety should be discussed in advance.
- S – Spirituality – Share something you are working on since your last check-in that is related to furthering your spirituality.

Understanding the difference between intensity and sexual intimacy is a key factor in adding value to sobriety. Addiction is all about the intensity of reaching a high but intimacy is the building block for a successful long term relationship.

Section VI

Tools for Managing Your Life

Chapter 11

What to Do When a Crisis Occurs?

You will have days that are less than glorious—maybe even many of them. Surviving is not enough. You have to create boundaries for yourself and spend time making recovery your priority. Don't be afraid to express your anger in a healthy way. Expressing anger is the necessary pathway toward eventual forgiveness. Admit your mistakes, set goals, and work toward them.

One of the most powerful ways to manage a stressful situation is by adapting the way you view it. The following skills are adapted from Dialectical Behavior Therapy, founded by Marsha Linehan, PhD, from the book, *Skills Training Manual for Treating Borderline Personality Disorder.* These tools have been shown to be effective in calming emotions and reducing stressful situations, which sometimes cause you to feel enslaved to substances or behaviors.

Act Dialectically

The word dialectic comes from the Greek word "dialectic" which takes the position that two seemingly opposite ideas can coexist, without diminishing the other. For example, it is possible to want to be sober and to still want to abuse substances. It is possible to love someone and be mad at them at the same time. It is possible to be happy about one part of your life and sad about another.

For the addict or trauma survivor, acting dialectically helps you get rid of black-and-white thinking, good or bad, right or wrong, perfect or imperfect, while considering the gray area may be a more sensible choice to balance your life. We accept the fact that people may not believe what we believe, may not act like we think they should act, and begin to practice a more middle path, balanced approach to life, feelings, and relationships.

When you are experiencing a craving, you can use the dialectic to surf your feelings like a wave in the ocean instead of acting on every impulse. Many people believe they need to act out when they experience a negative feeling. By using the dialectic, you simply ride the wave of the emotion, as it rises and increases in strength and then falls in a few moments.

Addicts and people who experience trauma look at things in terms of black and white, right or wrong, perfect or imperfect. When they experience a negative feeling, they suddenly want to make it go away and turn to abusing substances. Instead, think dialectically and realize there are also some positive things in life you can hold onto.

Actually, most of our lives we live in the gray areas. Dialectical Behavior Therapy shows us we can become willing to take our masks off and look at our lives in a new and different

DOI: 10.4324/9781003453185-17

way. It is a great relief when we realize there are alternative ways we can view our lives, our feelings, and our relationships, without having to make emotional decisions despite the consequences.

When you become triggered to use substances, think dialectically and you will realize that you can surf your urges like a wave in the ocean. The wave goes up and eventually comes down. So it is with our urges. If you can just step back and think about what else is true about the consequences of your actions. *Last time I abused substances I ended up in jail, wrecked my car, got a DUI, lost a relationship, or lost the tryout of my family.* Even in this moment of struggle, you can realize you have a choice. On the one hand, you want to use, while on the other hand, you want to remain sober.

Play the Tape Out

One of the most effective techniques for not reacting to emotional distress is the skill of play the tape out. Think of the tape as the progression of time that led to a slip or relapse. Sometimes, it can be a matter of hours, days, or months when we begin to feel disconnected from ourselves and reality by feeling restless, irritable, or discontent with life. When we play the tape out in our minds, we discover that things didn't turn out so well after we slipped or relapsed and we are back to square one, starting over again. So, we might say to ourselves, do I really want to go back to feeling withdrawals, going back to treatment, getting another DUI, suffering DTs again? Is it worth it for a moment's pleasure to experience the pain in the future?

Play the tape out can be used in the positive sense also. After someone has had a long-lasting sobriety and become triggered, they can think about how good it felt to be sober and whether they really want to go back to living life in their car or on the streets.

Exercise:

What would be your scenario to play the tape out that would prevent you from relapse?

_____

_____

What positive scenario can you envision from your sobriety that would help you?

_____

_____

Self-soothe

When a person is having a bad day or is under a lot of stress, he can use the self-soothe skill to help him calm down and tolerate the discomfort in a healthier way. People with addictions and trauma rarely find time to just relax in a healthy way. Some are so busy doing things for others; they fail to spend time self-soothing. Self-soothe helps a person stay grounded in their body and in the present moment and distracts them from the emotional pain they are experiencing.

To use self-soothe effectively, access all of your five senses: Vision, hearing, smell, touch, and taste. If you tend to overeat, food may not be your best choice for self-soothe.

One way to easily have access to elements for self-soothing is to create an SOS (self or soothe) box. Place objects for each of the five senses in the box so they will be readily available at all times.

Vision: Look at old magazines and choose a picture that reminds you of your safe place; an imaginary spot, like a river, mountain, lake, beach, or meadow, where you could simply relax with no cares in the world and appreciate the wonders of nature.

Hearing: Write down a list of your favorite songs and place them in the box, or leave your iPod in the box with your favorite tunes and listen when you need a break.

Smell: Place scented oils or scented candles in the box.

Taste: Collect coupons for your local ice cream store and treat yourself or simply place a small piece of chocolate, candy, or gum in the box for enjoying later.

Touch: Put a small, soft doll or teddy bear in the box or something smooth and comfortable to the touch.

Opposite Action

According to (McKay, M., Wood, J.C., Brantley, J.), our emotions are legitimate and valid and should not be ignored. It's when we react with our emotional mind that we have to be careful not to express our emotions in a negative way because acting on emotions can lead to destructive consequences. Another problem with acting on emotions is it intensifies the emotion. Instead of simply observing the emotion and letting it pass, acting on the emotion can lead to feeling consumed with anger, fear, anxiety, loneliness, or shame.

That's where opposite action comes in. Opposite action is about regulating our emotions. Being aware of what is happening in our body when we feel a certain emotion and working to calm the emotion down. According to (McKay, M., Wood, J.C., Brantley, J.), there are five steps to opposite action.

1. Acknowledge what you feel. Describe the emotion. Core emotions include fear, anger, sadness, disgust, joy, and excitement.
2. Ask yourself if there's a good reason to regulate or reduce the intensity of this emotion. Is your reaction justified or not justified? Justified anger would be someone punching you in the face for no reason. Unjustified anger is getting angry when people are doing something wrong that has nothing to do with you.
3. Is it overpowering? Does it drive you to do dangerous or destructive things?
4. Notice your body language and behavior that accompany the emotion. What's your facial expression, your posture? What are you saying and how are you saying it? What, specifically, do you do in response to the emotion?
5. Identify the opposite action.

   Anger: How can you relax your face and body, so it doesn't scream "I'm angry" or "I'm scared"? How can you acknowledge or ignore rather than attack? Justified opposite action is being kind to the person, build empathy, gently avoid the person, or work on accepting the situation. If you don't want to change how you feel, problem solve the situation, and change it. Distract yourself or express your anger without fuming with rage.

Depression: How can you convey confidence and vigor rather than depression? Opposite action is getting up and doing something to make you feel better, like exercise, a hobby, interacting with people who support you emotionally. Engage in life and get dressed up like you have some important places to go.

Fear: How can you move toward, not away from, what scares you? Solve the problem or run away when it's dangerous.

Guilt: If your guilt is justified, change your behavior to match your core values of honesty, integrity, or fidelity. Apologize for what you've done. Make a firm commitment not to do it again. If your guilt is not justified (you're being accused of doing something you did not do, for example), do what's making you feel guilty over and over. Remember that you are acting according to your own personal values and don't apologize for what you're doing.

Shame: When you have justified or unjustified shame and want to change it, don't act ashamed. Expose who you are to others and be truthful and vulnerable. The only way to rid yourself of shame is to talk about it in front of people who support you and will not shame you further. Everyone has shame and people will relate to your story and your feelings. When you don't want to change how you feel, keep your shame a secret and consider changing social groups where you can be more open and vulnerable.

Disgust: Fully commit to opposite action. Set a time frame to work on it. What were the consequences of acting on your emotions last time it happened? What are the possibilities that it could happen again?

Monitor your emotions. Notice how the original emotion may change or evolve. It helps you shift to a more appropriate reaction.

Set Goals

Goal setting is a necessary element of recovery. Without goals and dreams, something to look forward to, trauma survivors and people with addictions seem to wallow in their own misery with no direction in life and nothing to look forward to achieving. It's like walking through a forest with many paths and no map.

Goals need to be specific, measurable, realistic, and timely. If you want to lose weight, saying I want to lose 30 pounds is not a clearly defined goal. Say instead, I want to lose 30 pounds in the next 5 months and I will do that by exercising one hour per day and eating a low-carb diet of protein and vegetables.

There are many aspects of our lives we need to set goals for. Health, spirituality, career, self-improvement, social, and family. It's called *creating a life worth living*.

Life Worth Living Instructions

1. Along each line of the graph write the following, one along each line. You can customize these categories according to your own personal needs.

   i. Work
   ii. Play
   iii. Spirituality
   iv. Recovery

   1. Family/Intimate Relationships
   2. Social Relationships with friends
   3. Physical
   4. Education

2. Put a "10" at the end of each line on the outer edge of the circle at each point.
3. Fill in the middle where all lines intersect and mark as "zero."
4. Along each line, place a dot showing how much time you spend on each of these activities on a scale of 1–10.
5. Connect the dots.
6. Using another color, place a dot on each line representing where you would like to within the next year, balancing your life toward a life worth living.
7. Connect these dots.
8. On the back of the graph, write your goals for each category and how you plan to move from one dot to the next. For example, if you want to work less by 2 points so you have more time for play and relationships, what do you need to do to make this happen?
9. Write down the skills you can use to accomplish these goals.
10. Remember the SMART formula:

   S – Specific
   M – Measurable
   A – Attainable
   R – Realistic
   T – Timely

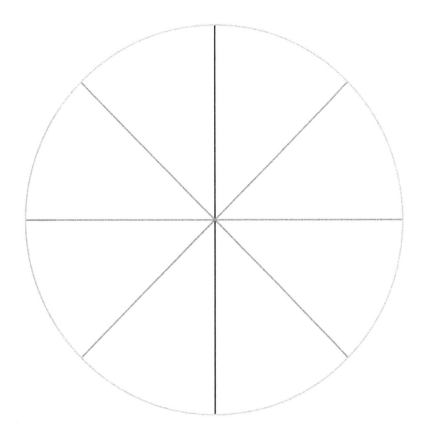

Pros and Cons

Benjamin Franklin hundreds of years ago used pros and cons to help him make better decisions. In Dialectical Behavior Therapy, one way we use this skill is in evaluating how we tolerate stressful situations and our reaction toward them. A person can use the skill for any decision they want to make and are having difficulty deciding. For example, an addict in treatment may be considering going to sober living or transitional living after discharge. He can use pros and cons to evaluate the advantages and disadvantages of moving back home to his normal environment or start over in a new place where he doesn't know anyone.

PROS	CONS

Chapter 12

Conclusion

Echkart Tolle says, "*Every addiction arises from the unconscious refusal to face and move through your own pain.*" It's difficult to be disciplined enough to not follow the masses into the morass of modern-day subjugation to technology, work, people, and emotions. The lure of instant gratification entices you in one direction, while our values and moral compass pull you in another. The journey to freedom is paved along the way with the promise of emotional stability rooted in spiritual values, mindfulness, character improvement, and a life of purposeful passion.

I have chosen to use Biblical sources in this book because the ethical principles it teaches form the original blueprint for all future generations. My hope is that the material in this book will serve as a stepping stone to your own personal journey to freedom, enlightened with a new perspective on all of the modern-day challenges and how you can personally overcome them while making yourself and your loved ones a priority in your life. Following the guidelines in this workbook and doing the exercises will insure you're adding value and purpose to your sobriety while avoiding relapses.

As Albert Ellis says, *the best years of your life are the ones in which you decide your problems are your own. You do not blame them on your mother, the ecology or the president. You realize you control your own destiny.*

To experience freedom, you must work through fear and self-doubt. Discover your passion and begin pursuing it today. Here's how… Decide what tasks you do daily that feel like play; things so easy to perform you don't really have to think about them much or prepare, where the flow of ideas and your expertise come naturally. Delegate as much as you can, and focus on what brings you joy. Find purpose and meaning in your sober life by being aware of how the distractions in this workbook affect you and take steps to work through your own journey.

Remember, your life's journey is to arrive at a set goal… a destination you want to reach in your life. When distractions and impulsivity become more important than what you're doing now, you've missed your life's purpose and pushed away the very people you've vowed to love and cherish. Your life's purpose has nothing to do with where you're going or what you are doing. It has everything to do with how free you're living in the present moment.

Living in the moment, with no resentments of the past and no worries about the future, is true freedom. Begin your journey today.

DOI: 10.4324/9781003453185-18

Assessment

Alcohol and Drugs

1. Have you ever felt you should cut down on your drinking or drug use?   Y   N
2. Have people annoyed you by criticizing your drinking or drug use?   Y   N
3. Have you ever felt bad or guilty about your drinking or drug use?   Y   N
4. Have you ever had a drink first thing in the morning to steady your nerves or get rid of a hangover (eye-opener)?   Y   N

Sex Addiction and Pornography Addiction

- Do you often find yourself preoccupied with sexual thoughts? (**P**reoccupied)   Y   N
- Do you hide some of your sexual behavior from others? (**A**shamed)   Y   N
- Have you ever sought help for sexual behavior you did not like? (**T**reatment)   Y   N
- Has anyone been hurt emotionally because of your sexual behavior? (**H**urt others)   Y   N
- Do you feel controlled by your sexual desire? (**O**ut of control)   Y   N
- When you have sex, do you feel depressed afterward? (**S**ad)   Y   N

How many times do you view Internet pornography per week?

_____

Approximately how long is each episode?

_____

How many times do you masturbate per week?

_____

How often do you have sex with your spouse or another person per week?

_____

Have you become less interested in partner sex since viewing pornography?

_____

Can you masturbate to climax without Internet porn?

_____

Do you have problems maintaining an erection when having sex with a partner compared to
Internet pornography?

_____

Have you escalated to pornographic genres that you find disturbing?

_____

Have you begun to question your sexual orientation since you began using Internet porn?

_____

Note

1 PATHOS by Dr. Patrick Carnes, Don't call it love, 1991, Bantam Books, NY.

References

Amsel, A. (1977). *Judaism and psychology*. New York, NY: Feldheim.

Anonymous. (1989). *White book of sexaholics anonymous*. SA Literature.

Basser. T. (2006). *Maharal of Prague Pirkei Avos*. Brooklyn, NY: Artscroll.

Bill, P., Todd, W., & Sara, S. (2005). *Drop the rock: Removing character defects*. Center City, MN: Hazelden.

Braun-Harvey, D., & Vigorito, M. A. (2015). *Treating out of control sexual behavior: Rethinking sex addiction*. New York, NY: Springer Publishing Company.

Brown, B. (2015). *Rising strong*. New York, NY: Speigel and Grau.

Cameron, J. (1992). *The artist's way: A spiritual guide to higher creativity*. New York, NY: Tarcher Perigee.

Carnes, P. (1991). *Don't call it love*. New York, NY: Bantam Books.

Ellis, A. (2000). *REBT resource book for practitioners*. New York, NY: Albert Ellis Institute.

Golden, B. (2017). *Healthy anger: A mind and body approach*. Memphis, TN: Counselor Magazine.

Hendel, H. J. (2018). *It's not always depression*. UK: Penguin Random House.

Hirsch, S. R. (1994). *Horeb: A philosophy of Jewish laws and observances*. New York, NY: Soncino Press.

Katehakis, A., & Bliss, T. (2014). *Mirror of intimacy*. Los Angeles, CA: Center for Healthy Sex.

Katz, A. J. (2009). *Addictive entrepreneurship*. Memphis, TN: Loyalty Publishing.

Laaser, D. (2008). *Shattered vows*. Grand Rapids, MI: Zondervan Publishing.

Linehan, M. (2017). *Practical DBT exercises for learning mindfulness, interpersonal effectiveness, emotion regulation and distress tolerance*. Oakland, CA: New Harbinger Publications.

Lewis, L. D. (1998–2004). Couples Company: http://www.couplescompany.com/Advice/Articles/Intimacy_Stages/default.htm.

Lieberman, D. (2008). *Real power*. Lakewood, NJ: Viter Press.

Lieberman, D. (2016). *How free will works*. Lakewood, NY: Viter Press.

Linehan, M. (1993). *Skills training manual for treating borderline personality disorder*. New York, NY: Guilford Press.

McKay, M., Wood, J. D., & Brantley, J. (2007). *The dialectical behavior therapy skill workbook.*, New York, NY: Ktav Publishing.

The Therapist's Assistant audiotape. (1996). Philadelphia, PA: Media Psychology Associates.

Twerski, A. J. (2002). *Self-improvement? I'm Jewish: Overcoming self-defeating behavior*. Brooklyn, NY: Shaar Press.

Twerski, A. J. (2017). *Teshuva through recovery*. Brooklyn, NY: Shaar Press.

Waldman, S. (2005). *Beyond a reasonable doubt: Convincing evidence of the truths of Judaism*. Nanuet, NY: Feldheim Publishers.

Index

For Product Safety Concerns and Information please contact our EU representative GPSR@taylorandfrancis.com
Taylor & Francis Verlag GmbH, Kaufingerstraße 24, 80331 München, Germany

www.ingramcontent.com/pod-product-compliance
Ingram Content Group UK Ltd.
Pitfield, Milton Keynes, MK11 3LW, UK
UKHW030829080625
459435UK00018B/600